MEET
JOE LIEBERMAN

THE MAN

THE HUSBAND

THE FATHER

THE SENATOR

THE CRITIC

THE BELIEVER

JOE LIEBERMAN:
The Historic Choice

The first and authoritative biography of the most
controversial candidate for Vice President

by *New York Times* bestselling author
Stephen Singular

BOOK YOUR PLACE ON OUR WEBSITE AND MAKE THE READING CONNECTION!

We've created a customized website just for our very special readers, where you can get the inside scoop on everything that's going on with Zebra, Pinnacle and Kensington books.

When you come online, you'll have the exciting opportunity to:

- View covers of upcoming books
- Read sample chapters
- Learn about our future publishing schedule (listed by publication month *and author*)
- Find out when your favorite authors will be visiting a city near you
- Search for and order backlist books from our online catalog
- Check out author bios and background information
- Send e-mail to your favorite authors
- Meet the Kensington staff online
- Join us in weekly chats with authors, readers and other guests
- Get writing guidelines
- AND MUCH MORE!

**Visit our website at
http://www.pinnaclebooks.com**

JOE LIEBERMAN

The Historic Choice

STEPHEN SINGULAR

WITH

Cherry Mosgrave *and* Paula Klaris

PINNACLE BOOKS
KENSINGTON PUBLISHING CORP.
www.pinnaclebooks.com

PINNACLE BOOKS are published by

Kensington Publishing Corp.
850 Third Avenue
New York, NY 10022

All Kensington titles, imprints and distributed lines are available at special quantity discounts for bulk purchases for sales promotion, premiums, fund raising, educational or institutional use.

Special book excerpts or customized printings can also be created to fit specific needs. For details, write or phone the office of the Kensington Special Sales Manager: Kensington Publishing Corp., 850 Third Avenue, New York, NY 10022. Attn. Special Sales Department. Phone: 1-800-221-2647.

Pinnacle and P logo Reg. U.S. Pat. & TM Off.

First Printing: August, 2000
10 9 8 7 6 5 4 3 2 1

Printed in the United States of America

ACKNOWLEDGMENTS

Thanks to Walter Zacharius, Jay Acton, Paul Dinas
and, of course, Reid Boates

Contents

8 CONTENTS

1

The Senator

Joe Lieberman could be called a walking contradiction. Not long ago the Democratic United States Senator from Connecticut and his wife, Hadassah, planned a Friday-night dinner party for some of their friends in Washington, D.C. The senator had to work late that evening and by the time he left the office, the winter sun had sunk below the horizon, the sky was dark, and the Jewish Sabbath had begun. It would run for the next twenty-four hours, until dusk on Saturday. As an Orthodox Jew, Lieberman did not drive during the Sabbath and also tried not to ride in cars, work, turn on or off electrical appliances, or talk on the phone. Now he was faced with a decision, a choice that affected no one but him. How should he get home? And should he try to be there in time for the start of the party?

It was five miles from the Senate on Capitol Hill to his Georgetown address, but he did not call a cab. Nor did he phone anyone to come pick him up, even though it was cold enough outside to snow. He put on his coat, buttoned it tight around his neck, and began walking briskly toward his house. It was better, his actions seemed to say, to be chilled and uncomfortable than to compromise his faith.

The senator, a trim, blond-haired, pink-faced man of fifty-eight, was in good shape. He seemed younger than his age and from certain angles he looked more Irish than Jewish. His eyes carried a brightness—a humorous twinkle, as if he were always remembering a joke—and something in his face conjured up a pixie or an elf. He was used to strenuous physical exertion and these long evening strolls kept the high color in his cheeks.

Back in 1988, when he'd taken on Lowell Weicker, Jr., the three-time and very popular Republican Senator from Connecticut, many people thought Lieberman had no chance. He'd turned to exercise as an ally. Right before debating Weicker, the challenger hit the deck and did a series of pushups—good ones with his chest touching the floor. This got his heart racing and his mind churning. It stirred him to project his voice and become a more forceful speaker. Gradually, he began to gain on Weicker in the polls but still trailed until he came up with a very successful TV commercial that portrayed the senator as a sleeping bear who snoozed through a number of important meetings. On election day, Lieberman took Weicker's job.

Five miles is a long distance, especially in cold weather, but Lieberman had made the trek before and looked forward to it on this Friday evening. He liked to view from street level the city that he'd lived in for the past dozen years, liked to watch the people as they moved past. He liked to think about his four children, two of them from his previous marriage, one from his wife's, and about passages in the Torah, and about his beloved New York Yankees. He liked to ponder the legislation and political issues he was working on and to consider the various points of view that others held in the Senate. He liked to examine his own positions and test them out for their strength and durability.

Lieberman enjoyed thinking just for the sake of thinking—he had, after all, written five books about public policies. Walking alone like this gave him the chance to do just that, think, and then make up his own mind about things. In his religious life, he often spoke with rabbis about ethical and spiritual matters yet rarely, almost never, about specific issues, preferring instead to reach his own conclusions. In his working life, he valued above all else his intellectual independence, his unpredictability, and following his own conscience.

Not only was he late for the dinner party, he was the last to arrive. His wife did not criticize him for his tardiness. She understood why he was the last to show up because he'd walked home on many a Friday night before. Hadassah (which is another word for "Esther" in Hebrew) shared her husband's faith and commitment to Orthodox Judaism. She kept a kosher home and sent their twelve-year-old daughter to a Hebrew academy. A Czech native, Hadassah had been born to two Holocaust survivors. Her father, Samuel Freilich, had been a slave laborer under the Nazis and her mother, Ella, had survived the concentration camp horrors of Dachau and Auschwitz. After the family fled to America in 1949, Samuel became a rabbi in Gardner, Massachusetts, where Hadassah grew up. As her life unfolded, she sometimes had trouble believing that both of her parents had almost been exterminated by German soldiers. Here, just a few decades later, she was the mother of one child she adored, a working woman, and married to one of the most respected members of the U.S. Senate.

It is no mystery that, like her spouse, Hadassah often

talked about the need for faith and the unlimited power of God.

In many ways, this blonde, attractive woman was as independent-minded as her husband—and she wasn't at all shy about challenging him when she felt it was necessary. Once, after attending a political function where he'd been lavishly praised by those sponsoring the event, he turned to her on the way home and asked, "How many truly great leaders are there in the Western world today?"

"One less than you think," she told him.

Senator Lieberman did not drive that Friday evening, but that didn't mean that he always followed every stricture of the Orthodox faith. He was too contradictory for that, and sometimes life was too complex. Occasionally, he worked on Saturdays or spoke on the phone. One weekend, he returned to the Senate chambers and cast seventy-five votes on pending bills. He was flexible enough to bend for what he saw as a higher purpose. Over the years, he'd approached a number of rabbis and asked them for help with resolving his dilemma of observing the Sabbath and fulfilling the demands of his very public job. They'd told him that there were generally only two exceptions to adhering to Jewish law. He could break the rules in order to save someone's life and he could also do this to serve the community. Voting on the Senate floor, the rabbis counseled, was allowed.

Lieberman's contradictions went beyond his religion and extended deep into his politics. He stood with the Clinton administration on gun control, abortion rights, gay rights, the environment, and various tax hikes, but some of his most important legislative efforts went against the party line. He supported vouchers, which would let parents use federal money to select schools for their children based on religious or other preferences—an idea abhorred by teachers' unions, one of the pillars of the Democratic establishment, but embraced by many Republicans. Lieberman was for limiting the damages a defendant could collect in a civil lawsuit, which angered many trial lawyers, another Democratic mainstay. He'd called for more military support for Kosovo, during the 1999 attack by the Serbs, than the Clinton administration had been willing to offer. And along with arch-conservative William Bennett, the former Secretary of Education, Lieberman had handed out "Silver Sewer" awards to entertainment companies that made what he thought were offensive movies, videos, and musical products. Hollywood is overwhelmingly Democratic and in recent years has been courted heavily by the party and by President Clinton. The entertainment capital of the world was not amused by the senator's actions.

Yet there were contradictions here too. Although he'd given out the Silver Sewers, Lieberman held considerable amounts of stock in two entertainment giants: CBS and Fox. Similarly, he often railed against campaign spending by corporate interests, but has accepted donations from them. He was a fervent believer in religion but supported only a moment of silence in schools—not prayer. And while he was a great backer of Israel, he'd also befriended Jordan's King Hussein and PLO leader Yasir Arafat. Lieberman's faith had taught him tolerance and accepting another's view of the world, even when he strongly disagreed with it, and he found that he used these tools as much in politics as when going to temple.

The senator had not built a great reputation as a legislator; there were no major bills with his name on them and several of his reform efforts had failed. Instead, he'd carved out a more unusual and provocative place for himself in Congress. He'd become, as the *Washington Post* put it, "a force of his own, taking on the role of the conscience of the Senate . . . with a passionate interest in issues involving morals and cultural values." Many Republican leaders had tried to cast themselves as the owners of America's moral high ground (and some had been revealed as shameless hypocrites), but Lieberman was the only one from the opposition party who'd been able to achieve this stature and hold on to it. By the mid-'90s he commanded the respect of both sides of the political aisle.

In 1998, his role expanded dramatically when he became the first Democratic Senator to come forward and publicly condemn the actions of President Clinton for his sex scandal with Monica Lewinsky. Lieberman called the chief executive's behavior with the young intern not merely inappropriate, but "harmful" to the nation and "immoral." In doing so, Lieberman faced opposition not only within his own party but also at a more intimate level. His wife heatedly argued against his making these comments, feeling that they were not proper for someone in his position and perhaps not proper for a Jewish man. He weighed her views, balanced them against his convictions, and did what he always did in such circumstances: He reached his own decision and acted on it.

He knew that he would be criticized both for moralizing and for grandstanding—and he was. Lieberman was the lone significant Democratic figure willing to accept these consequences and take such a harsh stance against the president. In subsequent days, espousing that the president's behavior did not "rise to the level of impeachable offense," the senator would vote not to remove Clinton from office but only to have him censured before the country. Some believed that within Lieberman's moral outrage other calculations were going on, and that by lashing out at Clinton when he did, he was really helping his longtime ally stay in office. To use the biblical phrase—and the senator had studied those ancient writings in depth—Joe Lieberman was exceptionally good at finding the eye of the needle and then passing through it.

One result of his outspokenness on the Lewinsky matter was that he accomplished something nearly unimaginable. Because of his strong family values' stance and moral fervor, the senator became one of the favorite Democrats of such Fundamentalist Christian evangelists as Reverend Jerry Falwell and his many followers, some of whom were at best uncomfortable with Judaism and at worst anti-Semitic. But Lieberman built bridges between people—he was called a "synthesizer" by many people—and he'd constructed this one over some very unlikely waters.

A much more prominent result of his denunciation of President Clinton came in August of 2000, on a very hot day in Nashville, when he was named by Democratic nominee Al Gore to be his running mate for the White House. Gore badly wanted to distance himself from Clinton and to align himself with someone who represented intellectual credibility, years of community service, and moral rectitude. Of five finalists for the job, and despite the obligatory public agonizing, Gore rather easily selected Lieberman and, thereby, placed the man who would be second-in-command under scrutiny as never before.

Not to worry, in the view of Jim Segaloff, Lieberman's old law partner in Connecticut. "Joe has lived his life," Segaloff told MSNBC on the day of the announcement, "as if he knew that one day it would be dissected and put under a microscope. When that happens, you'll still get just what you see from him in public."

Gore's decision was groundbreaking because for the first time ever a Jewish-American had been selected to become the vice-president—and just a moment away from assuming the chief executive's office. Never had someone with Lieberman's background risen so high on the national political ladder. An important barrier had fallen and minorities across the nation claimed it as a victory. Jesse Jackson, who'd had his own embarrassing and well-publicized issues over the conflicts between African-Americans and Jews, called Gore's selection "a political risk" but "a moral certainty."

Indeed, for the usually cautious Gore, picking the senator from Connecticut was a risk. Many commentators wondered if Lieberman's ascent would unleash latent anti-Semitism in segments of the country. As recently as 1998, a poll had found that 12 percent of the population believed that "Jews had too much power" and hate crimes against minorities had lately been increasing. The day after Lieberman became the vice-presidential candidate, Lee Alcorn, an African-American who headed the NAACP office in Dallas, made some extremely inflammatory comments, saying that blacks should be wary of people like the senator because Jews were mostly interested in money. Alcorn was instantly fired. On numerous websites around the United States, anti-Semitic statements, apparently from white racists, also showed up in chat rooms about Gore's running mate. There was danger and ugliness in these responses to Lieberman, but there was far more celebration and hope and the possibility that something new was unfolding on the American landscape, something the nation was ready for.

"The single biggest thing [about Lieberman's selection]," said Bill Schneider, a political analyst with CNN, "is that he restores religious values to public life."

"This is a brilliant move," the Fox News Network added. "He [Senator Lieberman] is living the kind of life many Republicans have been clamoring for."

Despite the challenges, fears, and certain attacks the nominee would be facing, Lieberman did not hesitate to accept Gore's offer. As was often the case in his public life, he immediately thanked God for his good fortune and then burst out, "Miracles happen." He quoted from Chronicles, he and Gore said a brief prayer together, and then the men began laying out battle plans for their campaign.

Hadassah Lieberman, echoing the deep historical experience of her family and her faith, also spoke publicly about her husband's new job.

"I feel privileged," she said, "to be joined by all the other immigrants who've come to America to find a better life. I feel that Holocaust victims are present today."

Throughout the media, a great deal was made about Senator Lieberman's Jewishness and whether he would campaign on the weekends and what he ate on a kosher diet and how he looked wearing a yarmulke. In a sense, all this was not germane to the central point of Liberman's faith, as it had shaped both his political career and his entire existence. What foods he consumed was of little real interest to the rest of America, but that he had been spiritually trained in a millennia-old tradition of critical thinking, independent analysis, fiercely debated ethical issues, flexibility, and striving toward living a good life was fundamentally important to what kind of man he had been and would be in office. His grounding in Judaism affected every personal and public decision he made.

The nominee was hoping that he would soon get to exercise his flexibility. If elected president, Al Gore would be inaugurated on January 20, 2001. That just happened to fall on a Saturday, but Senator Lieberman felt certain that he could make an exception to go to work that morning—without walking all the way there—and be sworn in as the second in command of his country.

2

The Early Years

If Joe Lieberman seems like a man of contradictions, so has his hometown of Stamford, Connecticut, always been a place of the same sort. On the one hand, long after its founding as a Puritan village in the 1640s, it remained very much an insular New England outpost. Yet, since incorporation as a city in 1893, it has been inexorably linked to the economic fortunes of New York City and to many of its residents. In the last twenty years, Stamford has become a major corporate headquarters itself and is now a study in contrasts. Its downtown is filled with both modern architecture and the free-standing, one-story buildings of private entrepreneurs. More than 100,000 people live in Stamford, many of them commuting to work in Manhattan. As Jane Jacobs pointed out in her seminal book *The Death and Life of Great American Cities:* "Cities are an immense laboratory of trial and error, failure and success, in city building and city design." The town Joe Lieberman was born into in 1942 fits this analysis, and its journey and evolution over the past six decades have run parallel to his own.

The Liebermans were a working-class family who

lived on Hamilton Avenue, one block away from the railroad station, in a house owned by Joe's grandmother. He
spent the first eight years of his life in modest circumstances, with a junkyard on one side of his home and a
multi-family tenement on the other. Joe's father, Henry,
a World War II veteran who was very proud of having
served his country, split fourteen-hour workdays between
a bakery and a liquor store that he owned. His wife, Marcia, remained at home to take care of her son and his two
younger sisters, Rietta and Ellen. Marcia was known for
the kindnesses she showed her neighbors and her extensive involvement in charities. In later years, Joe would
recall his father, who had not gone to college, vora-
ciously reading the *New York Times* each day and listening to classical music in his shop. The family was
orthodox and attended Congregation Agudath Sholom on
Strawberry Hill Avenue, where Joe is still a member.

   Family-dinner discussions were filled with current
events. Joe couldn't fathom why Adlai Stevenson, his favorite public figure, had lost twice to General Eisenhower
in the 1952 and 1956 presidential elections, and he
watched with curiosity the infamous Kefauver Senate
hearings on a black-and-white television. Like many
other boys, he had far more on his mind than politics.
His great goal in life, as he moved from Elm Street Elementary School to Burdick Junior High and then to
Stamford High, was to play center field for the New York
Yankees—to be the next Joe DiMaggio or Mickey Man-
tle. There was only one problem—he wasn't very good.
Simon & Schuster president Jack Romanos, who grew up
with Lieberman, told the *New York Times* that Joe was
placed on the periphery of the outfield so as not to cause
injury to himself or others.

   "He was," said Romanos, "awful."

Bob Kennedy, another high school classmate, whose father was then the mayor of Stamford, recalls a different athletic experience:

"I have to admit it—I never liked Joe Lieberman," he wrote in a column in the *Stamford Advocate,* where he is now the paper's sports editor. "It started when we were youngsters and played basketball at the old Jewish Community Center on Prospect Street. Joe never passed the ball. And he always seemed to go to his right."

Perhaps as telling, Kennedy got this annoying question more than once from his parents when he got into trouble: "Why can't *you* be more like Joe?" Rabbi Joseph Ehrenkranz, who formerly led Congregation Agudath Sholom and was Lieberman's rabbi, adds: "Joe played fair with all his peers and managed to be the darling of his teachers."

In truth, Joe did flourish at school. He was the natural in the classroom that he wasn't on a baseball diamond. In the ninth grade he was elected class president, and then repeated the feat as a sophomore and as a senior in high school. By his adolescence, the family had moved to Strawberry Hill Court, not far from where Bob Kennedy's family lived on Third Street. Bob couldn't help noticing that his friend was very good at working Bob's own parents, flattering them with inquiries and getting them to pay attention to him, to like and respect him even though he was still a teen.

"Another thing that bothered me was how Joe was always picking my father's brain," Bob recalls. "Joe would ask my father political questions."

After Lieberman was selected by Al Gore as his running mate, reporters nationwide descended on Stamford High School, looking for the obligatory yearbook. The 1960 "Golden Years" publication did not disappoint them. Lieberman was "Mr. Personality," assured of a successful future, and noted as someone who had a kind word for all. He was named most likely to succeed and most popular, and was honored as the person who did the most for the school, with his accomplishments on the debate team, in the choir, and in the class play. He was even voted King of the Senior Prom, but on the night of his coronation, the chair next to the 1960 Stamford High Queen was empty. The prom fell on the Sabbath, so Lieberman did not attend. (As a sophomore, he'd been voted "King of the Hop," but couldn't go because of the measles. His classmate Alex Lionetti substituted for him and served as consort to a pretty young queen named Vita. Alex and Vita were later married and still introduce Lieberman at political functions.)

The June 23, 1960, edition of the *Stamford Advocate* has a picture of Lieberman leading his 652 high school classmates into Michael Boyle Stadium for their graduation exercises. Naturally, he was the class valedictorian. The civil rights movement was stirring around the country, and leaders were emerging in both the South and the North who would push it forward in the years ahead. Lieberman, eighteen at the time, was aware of these developments and anxious to support them. This was well before young Americans were engaging in widespread social protests, but in his speech to the students, parents, and faculty on that sun-filled afternoon in the spring of 1960, he fervently urged his classmates to stand with him "in the vanguard of opposition to bigotry and discrimination." It was his first opportunity to reveal himself as an orator on political and moral issues, and he seized the chance. His words were far more meaningful than the homilies of the head of the local board of education, L.

Reed Clark, who told the seniors to "keep your eyes in the sky and both feet on the ground."

That fall he entered Yale University, amidst the country's immersion in drive-ins, sock hops, bowling alleys, and postwar prosperity. Change was in the wind: The Supreme Court had decided that segregation in education was unacceptable and illegal; Rosa Parks was defying the City of Montgomery, Alabama, with her refusal to ride in the back of a bus; and Arkansas governor Orval Faubus, who resisted racial progress in America, was stirring up rage in Little Rock. Abroad, the Cold War was quite hot and serious trouble was building in Indochina. Another war was coming and this one would be fought not just against the North Vietnamese on the other side of the world, but inside of each American.

If Stamford had nursed Joe's small-town dreams, Yale would greatly expand them. It shared a colonial history with his birthplace, but not much more. By 1718, Yale College was well established in New Haven and its intellectual hegemony was solidly in place. However, the city of New Haven experienced a series of immigrant upheavals, economic disasters, and a physical presence in stark contrast to the ivy walls of its university. New Haven was gritty and as the twentieth century unfolded, it looked increasingly industrial and aging, with rust at its core. The issues of town versus gown were never resolved. In 1954 New Haven mayor Dick Lee began serving the first of what turned out to be eight terms. With $300 million in development funds and help from Yale urban planners, he set out to remake the face of his city. Nearly forty years later, sections of New Haven are aesthetically appealing, but other parts seem incongruent, as if the planners had taken the city apart and were uncertain how to put it back together.

The New Haven Lieberman encountered in 1960 was in a state of perpetual undress, with projects that seemed to go on forever. Downtown was being made over with a new Macy's, a 300-room hotel, and other businesses. Despite Mayor Lee's best efforts, many of these prized enterprises would close down—a stunning urban defeat. People left New Haven for the suburbs, with the result that Yale itself became and remains the city's largest source of jobs, with over 10,000 employees.

The summer Joe arrived in New Haven, Senator John F. Kennedy was nominated by the Democratic Party to run for president. That November, Kennedy would defeat Vice-President Richard Nixon in one of the closest presidential races of all time—by an edge of a little more 100,000 votes out of over 68 million cast.

The first Catholic to be elected president, Kennedy inspired a great spirit of optimism and renewal in the country. With his epochal inaugural speech, a new era was launched on the Potomac. Young people everywhere felt they had a stake in their nation's destiny, and Joe Lieberman was no exception. But this particular Yale freshman's energy was compromised by something utterly foreign to him. This celebrated public high school boy from Stamford, the most likely to succeed in his class, was floundering, desperate to figure out his place and his identity in a sea of talented and voracious competitors. He was the first in his family to go to college, so no one at home could share his experience or offer much advice. He badly wanted to do well and to make his family proud of him, especially his father, who'd carefully saved enough to put Joe through Yale, but this, he quickly found, was a world far different, from far beyond, Stamford. The classes were much harder than he'd anticipated; he was surrounded by kids who were as bright and dedicated to studying as he was; and his feelings of specialness were severely put to the test. But he'd already developed the habits of discipline and commitment—of pushing himself when it was necessary, of finding out that he had other gears to call on—and he would not let down his father or himself.

Gradually things got easier and Joe began to do well. In December of 1962, he was named chairman of the *Yale Daily News*, a very prestigious position on campus that allowed him to articulate editorial policy on a wide range of social matters—both foreign and domestic. He threw himself into the political life at Yale, serving in the freshman and sophomore cabinet, becoming a registered Democrat, and becoming a member of the local chapter of the NAACP, the Young Democrats, the senior class council, and the Aurelian Honor Society. Joe was also a campus protester—of sorts. The 1964 class book shows a photo of him holding a poster that reads "UP With Girls." Yale did not begin admitting coeds until 1969.

As his political convictions began to take shape and he expressed them in different forums, some of his classmates found him to be guilty of a troubling college student sin: He was too serious, too *concerned*, for someone his age. He had moral and political *issues*, the relentlessness of which could alienate him from many of his peers. Edward Mattison, a Yale Law School classmate of Lieberman's told the *New Haven Register*: "Young people often don't think that deeply about politics, but I don't think Joe was really ever young. He was always better prepared and more knowledgeable than everybody else."

Yet others of his age found his seriousness endearing, if a bit weird. Many liked him for his inconsistent but often droll sense of humor. He belonged to a group called The Pundits, pranksters who joked about stuffy Yale traditions while sipping champagne on the library steps. But nothing could keep him from his pursuit of politics, which eventually connected him to the insular world of the Connecticut statehouse. During his undergraduate years at Yale, he managed to apprentice himself to two legendary local figures. He met John M. Bailey, longtime Connecticut Democratic chairman, at the state convention in 1962. This was like finding gold for Joe. Bailey had not only picked successful candidates and run winning elections in Connecticut; he had helped accomplish the unthinkable—elect a Catholic president in 1960.

He told John F. Kennedy that he would carry the state by 100,000 votes, a stunning prediction given that Adlai Stevenson had managed to lose the state to President Eisenhower in 1956 by 300,000 votes. The oldtimers who were there remember what Bailey pulled off on that November election night in 1960. As the working class-cities of Hartford, Bridgeport, and New Haven reported, the Kennedy margin swelled and he did take the state by Bailey's prescient margin of 100,000 votes.

And they remember Bailey in the undergrowth of the primary season as Kennedy struggled to secure the nomination. William Benton, a former senator from Connecticut, was providing financial support to the sputtering campaign of Senator Hubert Humphrey. Bailey politely informed Benton that if he hoped his own political future in Connecticut to be in any way meaningful, he would cease supporting Humphrey immediately. Senator Benton complied. Joe Lieberman loved hearing these stories again and again. They helped fortify his own future plans.

In 1963, Joe landed an internship at the Washington.

D.C., office of Senator Abraham Ribicoff, the most prominent Jewish politician in Connecticut. The former governor of that state, he had served two years in Kennedy's cabinet as the Secretary of Health, Education, and welfare before resigning to run for the Senate.

One day in Senator Ribicoff's office, Lieberman encountered a young woman named Betty Hass, who would become his first wife. She was more familiar with Washington than he was and opened up new connections and political vistas for him, pushing him to express and demonstrate his views about race and civil rights. Joe was soon marching with hundreds of thousands of others at the event that would culminate with Martin Luther King's "I Have a Dream" speech. In the fall of 1963, Lieberman traveled down to Mississippi to register black voters for a "mock" election that served as a precursor to the 1964 "Freedom Summer." When his friends wanted to know why he would take time off to do such a thing, he replied: "I am going because there is much work to be done. I am an American and this is one nation or it is nothing."

The young man's seriousness was not abating, as some had hoped it would, but growing deeper.

On November 22, 1963, when President Kennedy was assassinated in Dallas, the inner and outer landscape of all Americans was altered. Something was different now. Life was more complex and unpredictable than many young people had realized. Evil could appear at any moment, no one was really protected from it, and it could change things forever. For an earnest, politically sensitive young man like Lieberman, the loss was especially devastating. He believed in politics as the solution to many problems and he'd held the stylish Kennedys in great esteem. They were emblematic of everything youthful and

positive, and now JFK was gone and had been replaced
by the ultimate old-line Democratic politico: the Lone
Star state's Lyndon Baines Johnson. It was as if some
Texas crude had flowed into 1600 Pennsylvania Avenue
and no one could ignore the new difference. Nevertheless, in a move that would characterize Lieberman's entire career, he put aside his grief and disappointment and
managed a front-row seat at the transition from the
charmed politics of Martha's Vineyard to the lanky
power version of Texas' LBJ.

Lieberman was writing his Yale senior thesis on John
Bailey (which was published in 1966 by Houghton
Mifflin as *The Power Broker*). This kept him in Bailey's
company in Washington, and their association was good
for a ticket to the 1964 Democratic National Convention
in Atlantic City. The thesis was also good enough to be
awarded the Frank M. Patterson Political Science Prize,
which carried a stipend of $1,000. With a little money in
his pocket and a growing list of important names in his
phone register, the twenty-two-year-old was not merely
keeping his promise to make his father proud of him. He
was starting to thrive.

He applied to and was accepted by Yale Law School,
which was his way of hedging a bet. If a political career
were not in his future, he would at least always have a
way of making a living. Joe was already an intensely
practical man and nothing was more practical for someone with political ambitions than a law degree. After all,
many of the people he might eventually meet in politics
held the same piece of paper. It could only help him better understand arcane legislative matters. Doggedly attending law school, his nights most often spent in study
and his days in classrooms, he watched the country pass
through some of its most turbulent days from what might

be described charitably as a distance. Vietnam, not officially a "war," was escalating under LBJ. Protests
against Johnson's policies were erupting on one campus,
then hundreds more. Many undergraduates, and even
some law students, felt that there was little point in studying the rule of law if the president and his advisers were
going to push it aside and expand a war that many felt
was illegal and unconstitutional. Some of them took to
the streets, including Yale's own chaplain, William
Sloane Coffin. Others emerged as outspoken critics of
the Vietnam conflict, like Yale president Kingman Brew-
ster. For his part, Lieberman kept his nose inside his
books and made his grades. He opposed the war but he'd
been raised in a tradition of biblical study and caution
when it came to extreme thinking or actions. He was
moderate, he was ambitious, and he was determined not
to be derailed. While others were burning flags and
smoking marijuana, he was planting himself firmly
within the mainstream. His religion may have made him
an outsider from certain aspects of American life, but he
did not want to be removed from the rest of it. From an
early age, he shaped himself to join the power structure
of his country, not to ridicule or condemn that structure.

After graduating from law school in 1967, he announced his candidacy for the New Haven Board of Alderman, but was forced to withdraw when he did not
meet the residency requirement. Being an alderman was
a modest enough start, but Lieberman knew he would
have to work his way up through each step of the system.
He was willing to learn on the job. His idealism for public service was both real and deep. As his former law
partner, Thayer Baldwin, Jr., told the *New Haven Register,* "I think he was challenged by John F. Kennedy [to
the effect] that if you got involved and worked hard you

could make government work for people in a constructive way."

The epitome of two young, aggressive lawyers, Lieberman and Baldwin were employed for a time by a local firm. Then, rather brashly, the two started their own practice in the early 1970s.

"He had," Baldwin said of his former partner, "a broad reach across ethnic, racial and economic barriers, all of which were good skills in a city like New Haven."

The two partners began their practice in part because they had always seemed to agree on most things—with the notable exception of an earlier difference on which Lieberman felt he had to take a stand. Lieberman had backed Robert Kennedy for president in 1968, while Baldwin supported Eugene McCarthy.

Both young attorneys had survived that heart-smashing time to stay the course, to start their practice, and, in Lieberman's case, to move forward along a path that in retrospect might seem inevitable.

3

Local Politics: 1970–1988

The Connecticut General Assembly

Looking back on Joe Lieberman's career, observers might conclude that he was "destined" to reach executive office. "Determined" is a better word. He first showed that grit when running for an open Connecticut State Senate seat in 1970.

The Connecticut General Assembly is steeped in history: It has served as a legislative body since 1639. Originally, only white property owners could vote or hold public office. There was no separation of church and state; tax dollars were openly used to fund churches; and biblical laws were the foundation for Connecticut's early criminal statutes. Capital punishment not only existed, but was used against those who did not hold the extremely strict Puritan beliefs of the majority of the people. Dissenters—including religious heretics—were executed.

The Fundamental Orders, written to codify Connecticut's form of government, contained provisions that were to become the General Assembly and the state's most burdensome legacy. Under the Orders, every town, regardless of its size, was given two representatives in one voting chamber, which would ultimately become the House. Members of the state's other legislative chamber, which would become the Senate, were elected from the colony as a whole. This wasn't a problem in the late seventeenth century, but would become one in the future.

In the nineteenth century, when the state grew from an agricultural economy into a commercial center, some of the industries that still dominate Connecticut were founded, including guns, hardware, and machinery. After the Civil War, with immigrants pouring into the state, conditions sank to slum levels and a great division began to develop between political parties: rich, original sons of Connecticut or other parts of New England were Republicans; poor immigrants were Democrats. This divide changed before and during the Great Depression, but after World War II it reopened and created stagnation within the state government.

The General Assembly was continually hampered by partisanship and even during the prosperity of the postwar years it made little progress on the legislative front. In spite of revisions to the state Constitution, the town-based House overwhelmingly remained Republican and the Senate remained almost entirely Democratic. They were always at odds. Finally, the League of Women Voters sued Connecticut, and as a result, new districts were drawn. In 1965, the current General Assembly was born.

Five years later, Joe Lieberman became a state senator of Connecticut (population 3,000,000). He ran against the State Senate Majority Leader, Democrat Ed Marcus, who'd decided to try for a seat in the U.S. Senate. It was clear that Marcus would come to the State Senate if his bid for the U.S. Senate failed. Yet Lieberman was committed to winning, despite Marcus's wealth of experience and power in the General Assembly.

In part because of the historical difficulty of getting anything accomplished in the House, and in part because Connecticut's governor has the power to veto legislation that has passed through the General Assembly, most of the clout in state government rested (as it still does) in the hands of dominant governors like Abe Ribicoff. According to his February 23, 1998, obituary in the *Washington Post*, Ribicoff (who, incidentally, lost his first race for U.S. Senate against George Bush's father, Prescott Bush) might have attained the office of U.S. Attorney General under John F. Kennedy had not the president appointed his brother, Robert, instead. Ribicoff remained an idol of and mentor to Lieberman long after his tenure as Ribicoff's intern. The younger man had learned much from watching heavyweights of state government like Ribicoff, John Bailey, former Democratic governor Chester Bowles, and another Democratic Connecticut governor, John Dempsey, who held the office in 1970, the year Lieberman made his first political run against Ed Marcus.

The challenger was helped by the fact that his opponent had recently offended Governor Dempsey with some remarks. He also enjoyed the fervent assistance of numerous campaign volunteers, including an ambitious Yale Law student-politico named William Jefferson Clinton. Their paths would cross and re-cross many times in the future, and they would eventually alter one another's lives.

Lieberman defeated Marcus in the primary and won his seat in the General Assembly, where he served for the next ten years, six of them as Speaker. His political career was afloat, but the future would not be smooth sailing.

Two Lost Bids

In 1978, Lieberman lost his attempt to gain his party's nomination for lieutenant governor. Ella T. Grasso was elected governor, with William A. O'Neill as her lieutenant. When Grasso died in mid-tenure in 1980, O'Neill became governor. Under different electoral circumstances, this spot could have been Lieberman's, and it would have been a much more logical political stepping-stone than the next public office he held.

But he would lose another race before getting to that office—a loss that would have devastating effects on Lieberman's personal life. He chose to run for the open U.S. House of Representatives seat for the Third Congressional District against Republican Larry DeNardis. In 1980, as Ronald Reagan and other Republicans were swept into office, while Jimmy Carter and many Democrats were swept out, Lieberman lost. It wasn't by a large margin, with DeNardis taking only 52 percent of the vote to Lieberman's 46 percent, according to *The Almanac of American Politics,* but it temporarily smashed his hopes of attaining a national office.

This defeat hardly compared to what came next. In 1981, Lieberman, the devout family man, and his wife, Betty Haas, could not reconcile their differences and got divorced. Some problems were too overwhelming to negotiate or solve. There were conflicts inside the heart that religion had no pat answers for. The couple's children, Matthew, born in 1967, and Rebecca, born in 1969, were barely teenagers. Their emotional lives were of great concern to their parents, who were able to put aside their disagreements and work out an amicable custody arrangement.

The two, in fact, remained friendly and today one could call Ms. Haas a supporter of Lieberman. In his book *In Praise of Public Life*, published in 2000 by Simon & Schuster, he tells a revealing story about their relationship. After the senator denounced Clinton for his affair with Monica Lewinsky, he became a hot topic for call-in radio shows.

On one such show, a caller said that Lieberman had committed adultery during his first marriage (he had since remarried). It was subsequently asserted by another caller that the marriage had ended not because of adultery but because Betty Haas had died. Lieberman recalls, "Betty was so upset that *she* called in and told the talk-show host and his listening audience two things in no uncertain terms. First, like Mark Twain, the rumors of her death were greatly exaggerated. And second, she said she knew I never committed adultery."

State Attorney General

In 1982, Lieberman was elected Connecticut's first full-time attorney general with jurisdiction over the entire state (except over criminal cases, which do not fall under the purview of his office). According to the *Almanac of American Politics 2000*, Lieberman "took action against fake charities, crooked car dealers and gouging merchants." In a state that was essentially the headquarters of an insurance industry and other corporations, that many regarded as clogged by bureaucracy and indifferent to both workers and consumers, Lieberman went as far as the U.S. Supreme Court on behalf of an individual employee.

On November 7, 1984, Lieberman co-argued the case Estate of Thornton v. Caldor, Inc. before the Court. Donald E. Thornton, a manager in a Connecticut store owned by Caldor, Inc., was supposed to work on Sundays as part of his managerial position. But in 1979 he notified his employers that he could no longer do so, referring to the Connecticut statute on the topic: "No person who states that a particular day of the week is observed as his Sabbath may be required by his employer to work on such day. An employee's refusal to work on his Sabbath shall not constitute grounds for his dismissal."

Thornton's bosses offered to transfer him to a Massachusetts location that was closed on Sundays or to demote him to a nonmanagement position where he worked, while lowering his pay. He rejected both options and was demoted to a clerical job in his store in Connecticut. Two days later, Thornton resigned and filed a grievance with the State Board of Mediation and Arbitration, stating that he had been dismissed from his position in violation of state law.

The board ruled in support of the grievance and ordered Caldor, Inc., to reinstate Thornton in his original position. The Connecticut Superior Court agreed as well. But the Connecticut Supreme Court disagreed with the statute itself, on the basis that it did not have a secular purpose and served to endorse the religious practice of celebrating the Sabbath. It reversed the ruling.

The U.S. Supreme Court ultimately upheld the Connecticut Supreme Court's ruling. Thornton himself did not live to see the end of this long judicial battle, in spite of the best efforts of the attorney general's office. Although he lost, Lieberman had fought hard for the right of the individual (in this case, a Christian individual) to commemorate his Sabbath, a fight that mirrored Lieberman's own convictions about observing the Sabbath.

As attorney general, Lieberman was popular with his constituents. A list of the "highlights" of his years in office (put out by the attorney general's office) reads like the record of a people's advocate and indicates his strong stance on the environment, consumer protection, child support, and affirmative action. According to this list, Lieberman:

- defeated a proposal by the City of Springfield, Massachusetts, to dump millions of gallons of raw sewage into the Connecticut River;
- defended Connecticut against a plan by the City of New York to route trucks carrying radioactive waste across Long Island Sound and through Connecticut in order to avoid New York;
- won a fine of $3.6 million against the Rolfite Corporation, formerly of Shelton, Connecticut, for hazardous-waste violations;
- fought for a $2.2 million fine against the Upjohn Company for numerous water pollution violations;
- collected thousands of dollars in fines from a number of automobile dealerships engaged in deceptive advertising;
- mounted several challenges against companies involved in products that posed a health and safety risk to children;
- cracked down on health clubs that defrauded hundreds of consumers;
- formed the Public Charities Union to focus on charitable-solicitation fraud (the unit has successfully brought legal action against a number of "boiler room" charity frauds and has put them out

of business and collected restitution for legitimate charities);
- defended the state's new car Lemon Law against auto maker challenges and initiated legal action to collect new cars from automakers after consumers complained about their "lemons";
- brought the attorney general's office into the utilities field on the side of consumers for the first time;
- supported consumers against the cable television industry and the FCC, attempting to maintain rate regulation and other consumer-protection measures threatened by government deregulation;
- saved ratepayers $800,000 yearly through reduction in the interest rate charged customers making late payment of Northeast Utilities bills;
- substantially improved laws governing child-support collections;
- in 1986–1987, collected nearly $28 million in overdue child-support awards;
- initiated an aggressive affirmative action program within the office;
- brought legal action against illegal insurance operations;
- improved Connecticut's drunk-driving laws.

In 1982, the year he became attorney general, Lieberman met his next wife. Divorced herself with a small son, Hadassah Freilich was an Orthodox Jew originally from Prague, Czechoslovakia. Both of her parents had survived the Holocaust. Her mother was held in concentration camps near Dachau and Aushwitz and her father was forced to work in Nazi labor camps. After the family came to America in 1949, Hadassah's father served as a rabbi in Gardner, Massachusetts, where she grew up surrounded by Orthodox Judaism. In 1983, she and Lieberman were married and their daughter, Hana, was born in 1988, the same year that Lieberman's career would take another great step forward.

In a race that almost no one expected him to win, he captured the junior seat in the U.S. Senate next to Christopher J. Dodd, the Democrat who'd succeeded Lieberman's old mentor, the estimable Abe Ribicoff. Now Lieberman was following the path of an early political teacher and hero—while starting to make headlines of his own.

In 1988, midway through his second term as attorney general, Lieberman was urged to run for the U.S. Senate against the ever-voluble, three-term Republican incumbent Lowell P. Weicker, Jr. Intitially, this was a race that few people thought Lieberman could win. Early polls put him twenty-five percentage points behind Weicker, who had proven himself early on to be strong in matters of independent thought and speech.

Yet beneath the numbers lay some other interesting statistics. Lieberman was already taking a hard look at the 1990 Connecticut governor's race. At this point, the polls showed him running third, so perhaps his political future lay elsewhere. But the most intriguing fact was that fewer than half of all voters surveyed felt that Weicker actually deserved reelection. He was widely perceived as lazy, complacent, and dismissive of potential opponents. He was also regarded as self-absorbed—always dangerous for a politician. Weicker's campaign slogan was "Nobody's man but yours."

Lieberman, to emphasize Weicker's alienation from the voters, waggishly turned this slogan into "Nobody's man but his."

In none of his three senatorial campaigns had the incumbent enjoyed a large victory. He'd won a three-way race in 1970 with 42 percent of the vote. Six years later, against a weak candidate, he mustered only 58 percent, and in his last race, in 1982 against Representative Toby Moffet, he captured only 50 percent of the ballots. His winning margin was attributed to the 4 percent of the vote received by a third-party candidate. Weicker had hung on for three terms despite the fact that Democrats held a huge registration advantage in Connecticut and the senator had alienated much if not most of his traditional Republican base.

Lieberman's 1980 congressional defeat still haunted him, having taught him to take nothing for granted in electoral politics. You needed to work harder, longer, and smarter to have a clear chance at winning, he repeated to himself.

Weicker took very little notice of the determined Lieberman. Is this best Connecticut Democrats could do, his demeanor seemed to say, to run their low-profile attorney general against *me*? He professed not to be worried at all. The incumbent should have realized that while he, Weicker, had been off in Washington the last eighteen years, Joe Lieberman had been building a solid foundation at home. In 1986, Lieberman had topped the statewide democratic ticket, winning reelection by over 600,000 votes.

Lieberman saw a possible benefit even if he were to run and lose against Weicker: A decent showing would raise his profile in Connecticut for the 1990 governor's race. This amounted to a free shot, because even if he lost, it would be to a worthy opponent *and* he would retain his post as attorney general. The late Speaker of the House Tip O'Neill was fond of saying that all politics sprang from opportunity. Lieberman had something better than a mere opportunity. This was a freebie—an experiment in running a Senate election—and those were hard to find. While he wondered what he might have to lose by running, he couldn't have known, or even guessed, how much dissatisfaction the Connecticut electorate was harboring for Lowell Weicker.

A loner who said what he felt and did what he wanted, the senator never studied the polls to make up his mind about an issue—an admirable trait, but also a dangerous one. He'd arrived on the national stage when, as a first-term Republican senator, he'd criticized President Nixon during the Watergate hearings. Later he would lambaste President Reagan for bombing Libya. And his pro-choice position on abortion put him out of sync with many Republicans.

Conservatives like William F. Buckley, Jr., loathed Weicker and were committed to getting rid of him, even if it meant electing a Democrat. In fact, Buckley formed a political action committee called Buckleys for Lieberman (BUCK-PAC). Its initial plan was to ask all 12,000 people in Connecticut named Buckley to send BUCK-PAC a contribution to help defeat Weicker. Buckley's house organ, *The National Review*, continued the barrage. After labeling the senator "imperially obnoxious," the publication quoted columnist James Jackson Kirkpatrick as saying: "He has yet to hear one human being utter one respectful, let alone admiring, let alone affectionate word about Weicker."

The magazine charged that Weicker was continually looking for "keener formulations that express his character" and claimed that he'd once portrayed himself this way: "I've always been the turd in the punch bowl." *The National Review* lauded this self-appraisal as an "artistic triumph of self-description."

As the campaign progressed, the piling-on continued. Syndicated columnist George F. Will, no fan of the senator, weighed in with the kind of solemnity that he usually employed only when writing about baseball: "The challenge for anti-Weicker Republicans is to relate their rebellion to something more than ideological fastidiousness. It should even be larger than the correct belief that Weicker's political style involves too much subtraction from public civility. The rebellion should be based on this idea: there must be some limits to the disregard of Party loyalty, some boundaries, however broad, to the naked individual entrepreneurship that characterizes political careers like Weicker's."

During the campaign, Lieberman employed what he called a left-right strategy. He appealed to the left when he contended that Weicker had been weak on consumer and environmental issues, two areas where the challenger had received much favorable coverage as attorney general. But Lieberman also appealed to the right because on crime and foreign policy, his views were generally more conservative than Weicker's.

The upstart criticized Weicker for missing important Senate votes because he was out giving paid speeches to lobbyists. And Lieberman aired a series of strikingly effective television commercials that showed Weicker as a large hibernating bear, sleeping instead of working for his Connecticut constituents. In his 1995 autobiography, Weicker admitted that that he was slow to respond to the attacks, but he also revealed that seven years after the 1988 campaign, Lieberman's tactics still stung. Weicker felt that he'd worked hard for his state and its citizens, and in retrospect he was angry.

"Lieberman," said Weicker, "ran an extensive, nasty

ad against me, in line with the current view that a negative campaign is the only way to go."

Weicker was most upset by the notion that he'd missed key votes to give paid speeches: "Absenteeism was never a problem of mine. . . . I believe I put in more time on the Senate floor than any other member."

But he did admit to running a "sloppy, lazy" campaign against Lieberman: "I didn't campaign physically. I disregarded the one-on-one style that had been so successful."

Weicker's campaign, or lack of one, played right into Lieberman's strategy of depicting the incumbent as lazy, self-absorbed, and self-satisfied. A late October appearance by the senator at Fairfield University demonstrated just how much trouble he was in. As George Bush, the soon-to-be president, introduced him to the audience, Weicker, to his astonished embarrassment, received a round of loud boos. The twenty-five-point lead was long gone. A few days later, Lieberman won by 10,000 votes.

4

The U.S. Senate Years

The 1988 election that brought Joseph Lieberman to the U.S. Senate had not been as kind to the Democratic Party as a whole. For the third election in a row, the Republican presidential ticket had defeated the Democrats. George Bush defeated Michael Dukakis by a wide margin, wielding "the L word" against Dukakis like a bludgeon.

The Democratic Party had to change, or risk dying out.

The Birth of the New Democrat

In fact, change had already begun in 1985, with the formation of the Democratic Leadership Council, or DLC. The mission of the new organization was to create a more viable Democratic Party, one that would more accurately reflect the concerns of mainstream Americans and, above all, have a fighting chance of winning elections. Frustrated by the dominance of the liberal wing of the party, several centrists formed a loosely organized group distinctly separate from the Democratic Party yet with membership left open to any elected Democrat. On February 28, 1985, the DLC was unveiled at a Capitol Hill press conference. On hand were all the founding members: Sen. Lawton Chiles (D-Fl.), Gov. Chuck Robb (D-Va.), Sen. Sam Nunn (D-Ga.), Gov. Bruce Babbitt (D-Az.), and Rep. James R. Jones (D-Ok.). The group's first president, who has remained in that position since, was Al From, long an inside operative among Democrats on the Hill.

In a recent article in the DLC magazine *The New Democrat*, From recalls the group's motivation:

"When we formed the DLC in 1985 to develop a new, modern agenda for our party, we had two goals in mind. First, we hoped a New Democrat candidate would ride that agenda all the way to the White House, ending our party's long losing streak in presidential elections. Second, we hoped our agenda would transform the Democratic Party from top to bottom and help return it to its rightful place as America's majority party."

The immediate result was more modest. In the summer 1995 issue of *Political Science Quarterly*, Jon F. Hale analyzed the ongoing shift in the Democratic Party. His article, "The Making of the New Democrats," says that the DLC "developed a dualistic nature during its first four years. It was part forum for elected officials interested in discussing party positions on policy and in creating an impression in the public mind of a temperamentally moderate party, and it was part movement for those elected officials specifically interested in moving the party message to a more centrist position." According to Hale, DLC membership grew from an initial count of 70 to nearly 200 by 1994.

However, the election of 1988 brought fresh disaster for the Democrats. Michael Dukakis, the Democratic candidate for president, was unable to effectively counter

Bush's accusations of outdated "card-carrying" liberalism. Democratic candidates for local and state-wide office had absolutely no coattails on which to rely. Joseph
Lieberman was one of the few Democrats to prevail in
this election, and he won by a sliver of a margin—only
10,000 votes.

The painful defeat forced Democrats to take action.
DLC policy director Bruce Reed remembers that post-
election moment: "The DLC settled in for the long haul
after 1988. It was good for the organization."

The Progressive Policy Institute (PPI), a think tank
closely allied with the DLC, was formed in 1989.
Through DLC conferences and PPI policy statements, the
word was spread: The Democrats' recent defeats were
due to Americans' perceptions of the party as the home
of outdated left-wing orthodoxy, tax-and-spend bureau-
crats, and soft-on-crime social welfare advocates. There
was no point arguing that the perception was unfair; the
party had to deal with its existence and overcome it. It
wasn't enough to simply shake off the label, as Dukakis
had tried to do. There had to be a coherent new philosophy to put in its place.

That new philosophy was first unveiled in 1990, at
the DLC's annual conference, when the term "New Democrats" was first mentioned prominently. The philosophy
of New Democrats is currently defined by the DLC thus:

> New Democrats are the modernizers of the pro-
> gressive tradition in American politics. We believe in
> the traditional values that have always propelled the
> Democratic Party and we believe that the best way to
> further those values in a new era is to modernize our
> policies and programs to keep up with the changing
> times.
>
> Our enduring purpose is equal opportunity for all,

special privilege for none. Our public ethic is mutual responsibility. Our core value is community. Our outlook is global. And our modern means is an empowering government that equips people with the tools they need to get ahead.

New Democrat policies transcend the stale left-right debate and define a Third Way for governing based on progressive ideas, mainstream values, and innovative solutions that reflect changing times. New Democrat ideas that have become law include national service, work-based welfare reform, charter schools, community policing, an expanded earned-income tax credit, and market incentives for environmental protection.

This new philosphy precisely dovetailed with Lieberman's beliefs and philosophy. This was a new, less paternalistic approach to governance, one that stressed personal responsibility. The government would still participate in the economic and social life of the country, but on a partnership basis. Government wasn't the enemy or the only answer.

The 1992 election was the first real test of the New Democrats. Could they convince Americans that "the l-word" no longer applied to them? At campaign headquarters, James Carville now-famously posted a sign to remind workers of the most important message to get out: "It's the economy, stupid."

This was a message that resonated with voters, and Bill Clinton broke a long White House losing streak for the Democrats. But once they were in office, the message seemed to get lost. After almost six months of a Clinton presidency, Richard Benedetto reported in a *USA Today* article (6/3/93): "President Clinton won the 1992 election by convincing voters he was a 'new kind of Democrat,' but since taking office, Clinton's appointments and policies have appeared overwhelmingly liberal, triggering GOP talk of winning the Senate in 1994 and the White House in 1996."

As Clinton drifted away from the New Democrat line, Lieberman and other DLC stalwarts prodded him back toward the center. In the run-up to the 1994 midterm elections, an article in the *Wall Street Journal* (10/28/94) singled out Lieberman for his staunch moderation:

"Sen. Joseph Lieberman actually is what Bill Clinton promised to be, a 'different kind of Democrat.' Now Sen. Lieberman is cruising toward re-election while President Clinton and a host of congressional Democrats are in trouble.

"Could there be a lesson here?

"There could indeed, the freshman senator argues. . . . The lesson, as he sees it, is that voters really meant it in 1992. They really wanted change, but pragmatic change, not a return to old-fashioned liberalism. They wanted practical answers to the problems that trouble their daily lives. They saw politics, he says, as 'a game, a tug-of-war with no particular results.' But they didn't want a game, they wanted solutions. They still do."

After the Republican Revolt of 1994, the Democratic Party had to regroup. Lieberman stepped into the chairmanship of the DLC, a role he's maintained since. As chairman, Lieberman has been one of the key figures in shaping a new political agenda called The Third Way. As described by the DLC, "the 'Third Way' is a new political synthesis that combines economic dynamism and social justice. It looks beyond the sterile choice between big government and no government and envisions an enabling government that equips citizens and local communities to solve their own problems."

The New Democrats' success helped the center-left movement spread beyond U.S. borders; both Prime Minister Tony Blair of Britain and Chancellor Gerhard Schroeder of Germany incorporated Third Way tenets in their successful campaigns and the resulting administrations. In April 1999, President Clinton and the DLC hosted a globally focused discussion called *The Third Way: Progressive Governance for the 21st Century.* Among those participating were Blair, Schroeder, Prime Minister Wim Kok of Holland, and Prime Minister Massimo D'Alema of Italy.

Their guiding philosophy, as presented in the DLC website:

"The Third Way philosophy seeks to adapt enduring progressive values to the new challenges of the information age. It rests on three cornerstones: the idea that government should promote equal opportunity for all while granting special privilege for none; an ethic of mutual responsibility that equally rejects the politics of entitlement and the politics of social abandonment; and, a new approach to governing that empowers citizens to act for themselves."

The growth and evolution of the New Democrat principles reflect the longstanding values of Lieberman, one of the engineers of that growth. Lieberman's Senate record demonstrates his commitment to this philosophy.

As Lieberman puts these principles into action, he's garnered some criticism from Democratic colleagues and former allies. One reelection endorsement Lieberman did *not* receive in 1994 was that of the Caucus of Connecticut Democrats, representing the liberal faction of the state party. (Ironically, Lieberman was one of the founders of the group when he served in the Connecticut legislature.)

After the 1997 campaign finance hearings, the largely

positive response to Lieberman's work included a less generous assessment, described in a *New York Times* article: "Some in his own party say, on condition of anonymity, that Connecticut's junior senator is increasingly conservative and something of a moralizer."

Even so, Lieberman's effectiveness and civility are notable on the Hill.

Budget/Spending/Welfare

New Democrats believe in fiscal discipline, a progressive tax system free of special-interest subsidies, and government budgets that emphasize investments in the country's long-term well-being.

Stressing the need for the United States to compete in a global marketplace, Lieberman supported both the North American Free Trade Amendment and the General Agreement on Tariffs and Trade. This put him at odds not only with many of his fellow Democrats, but also with many traditional allies of the party, such as the AFL-CIO.

Lieberman crossed party lines to vote for the capital gains tax cut as well as a moratorium on Internet taxes; he continued to work with colleagues on both sides of the aisle to achieve a balanced budget. In 1993, he introduced the Equity Expansion Act, which protected accounting standards that allowed stock options to be deducted from profits. Cash-short new businesses often use stock options to compensate workers willing to gamble on the new company. One could argue that this bill helped contribute to the explosive growth of the new-technology market and the corresponding rise in the stock market.

In the 103rd Congress, he co-sponsored, with Sen. Jay Rockefeller (D-W.Va.), the Product Liability Fairness Act, which would have produced uniform standards for civil liability lawsuits. The act provided for an expedited judgment and alternative resolution process (including penalties for parties who refused to settle and lost in court); national standards for time limitations on suing, seller liability, and punitive damage amounts; and assurance of a complete defense in cases where the claimant was under the influence of alcohol or drugs and was more than 50 percent responsible for the harm.

The bill did not pass and—in the midst of 1994's spate of corporate downsizing—American business noticed. As reported in a *Washington Post* article (7/10/94), John Endean of the American Business Conference named the bill's defeat as one factor in the corporate-sector reluctance to expand and create new jobs.

With a seat on the Small Business Committee, Lieberman has in the current Congress co-sponsored five bills, including the following:

THE SBIC TECHNICAL CORRECTIONS ACT

The Small Business Investment Company (SBIC) program is vital to our fastest growing small companies that have capital needs exceeding the caps on SBA's loan programs, but are not large enough to be attractive to traditional venture capital investors. This legislation makes five technical changes to the program, ranging from improving the incentive for SBIC's to loan money to small companies to structuring a fairer formula for determining whether companies of the same revenue size can quality for SBIC financing.

THE MILITARY RESERVIST SMALL BUSINESS RELIEF ACT

This bill helps small businesses whose owner, manager, or key employee is called to active duty. The legislation was designed as a direct result of the conflict in Kosovo, but the act also applies to future contingency operations, military conflicts, or national emergencies.

THE COMMUNITY DEVELOPMENT AND VENTURE CAPITAL ACT

This legislation has three parts: a venture capital program to funnel investment money into our poorest communities, a program to expand the number of venture capital firms that are devoted to investing in such communities, and a mentoring program to link established, successful businesses with businesses and entrepreneurs in stagnant or deteriorating communities in order to facilitate the learning curve.

New Democrats believe government should promote resources for helping working families lift themselves out of poverty

In the October 1994 *Wall Street Journal* article cited earlier, Lieberman said, "Welfare reform embodies so many of the values that are so important to the New Democrats, the willingness to take on old programs that haven't worked . . . the idea that we aren't just a society of rights gone wild, but of responsibilities."

In addition to supporting the 1996 Welfare Reform Act, Lieberman wrote provisions of the law that assist teenage mothers, discourage out-of-wedlock pregnancies, and help states that move welfare recipients into self-supporting jobs. Another proposal would set up Individual Development Account (IDAs) for low-income families. These special tax-free savings accounts match deposits dollar for dollar by offering government tax credits to participating banks; in turn, the IDA must be used to pay for education, purchasing a home, or starting a new business. In February, Lieberman introduced the Savings for Working Families Act to broaden the IDA program on a national scale.

New Democrats support efforts to spread productivity-enhancing technologies to every industry, community, and family, while equipping every American with the knowledge, skills, and other resources needed to succeed in the New Economy.

Lieberman believes in leveraging federal dollars to create economic growth. He favored investment in two innovative programs: the Defense Advanced Research Projects Agency (DARPA), which provided funding for high-risk, long-term research; and Sematech, a partnership between the semiconductor industry and the U.S. government. This alliance between public government and private enterprise helped expand the high-tech sector, and also allowed American defense technology to keep up with a fast-changing world. *Electronic News* (5/12/97) covered a speech Lieberman gave to a group of American scientists and engineers. In the speech, Lieberman said:

"For almost a decade, American military planners have foreseen dramatic changes in military strategy, what some call a revolution in warfare. I believe a revolution has indeed begun, but it will be shaped by powerful forces emanating from beyond the domain of warfare. These forces are information technology and the development of a global economy.

"If you accept, as I do, that we are undergoing such a revolution in military affairs, then we must construct our defense policies in accordance with the rise of information technology and the influence of the world market. No longer will the Department of Defense be able to practice a kind of military socialism in a sea of capitalism."

Defense and Foreign Affairs

New Democrats believe in progressive internationalism: a U.S. leadership role, in conjunction with allies and multilateral organization, aimed at promoting political and economic freedom, resolving dangerous regional conflicts, and dealing with new threats to peace and security like terrorism, cyber-warfare, and chemical and biological warfare.

One of Lieberman's biggest areas of difference with many of his more partisan colleagues is his strong support of the military. As a member of the Armed Services Committee, Lieberman has voted to increase defense spending, including funds for the missile defense system. Lieberman is the ranking Democratic member of the Airland subcommittee, and also serves on two other subcommittees: Emerging Threats and Capabilities, and Strategy.

Early in his Senate career, Lieberman made a strong stand in favor of military action. In early 1991, as the Iraqi invasion of Kuwait unfolded, the Bush White House asked Lieberman to co-sponsor a resolution authorizing the president to wage war. Lieberman later told the *New*

Republic (2/4/91) that his response was that he'd be "proud" to offer his support.

Once the bill came up for a vote, Lieberman worked hard to persuade Democrats to cross party lines in support. Lieberman said, "I couldn't find enough hard Democratic support to make me comfortable. Senator Albert Gore of Tennessee, for example, was uncertain." Lieberman kept pushing.

According to the *New Republic* article:

"After the vote, Lieberman was summoned to Dole's office to meet Iraqi Ambassador Mohamed al-Mashat. Asked what could be done for peace, the ambassador urged senators to fly to Baghdad as a peace delegation. 'For our answer,' said GOP Senator John Warner of Virginia, 'we'll yield to our leader, Senator Dole.' Dole said nothing. Moments later, a congratulatory phone call came from Bush. Dole spoke first, then put Lieberman on the line. 'This is the first call I've made,' Bush said. 'I know it was a tough vote. I appreciate your leadership.' Lieberman said he'd be wary of giving the power to go to war 'to some people.' But not to Bush."

During the 1998 air strikes against Iraq, Lieberman became a forceful and articulate supporter of the administration's actions. In a discussion on "The NewsHour" with Jim Lehrer (2/10/98), Lieberman argued for decisive action against Hussein and his refusal to permit U.N. weapons inspections:

"I don't say this believing it's easy and I don't say it believing it's going to happen tomorrow. You saw how resilient he was during and after the Gulf War, but . . . just as we drew the line in 1991 on his invasion of Kuwait, we've got the draw the line and send a larger message to other countries around the world that we're not going to tolerate rogue nations developing chemical and biological weapons capacity with which they can damage or blackmail a lot of the rest of the world."

As Clinton's response failed to gather support, Lieberman continued to push for a Senate resolution of support. In a story on CNN.com (2/13/98), Lieberman spoke out against the actions of Russian Defense Minister Igo Sergeyev. The senator called Sergeyev's dressing-down of U.S. Defense Secretary William Cohen, and a threat of disrupted defense ties as a result of any U.S. strike, "outrageous, uncalled for, and unnecessarily provocative."

He was one of twenty-seven senators who signed an October 9, 1998, letter, read into the Congressional Record, urging Clinton to "take necessary actions (including, if appropriate, air and missile strikes on suspect Iraqi sites) to respond effectively to the threat posed by Iraq's refusal to end its weapons of mass destruction programs."

While running for president in 1996, Senator Bob Dole, in an interview on "The NewsHour" with Jim Lehrer (4/17/96), spoke of Lieberman's assistance "carrying the ball on the Senate side" in an attempt to lift the arms embargo and allow Bosnian Muslims to defend themselves. Once it became clear that that approach wouldn't work, Lieberman supported action on behalf of the Kosovars. In a debate with Patrick Buchanan on "Meet the Press" (4/25/99), Lieberman said:

"Ronald Reagan did not lead us to victory in the final battles of the cold war for us, less than a decade later, to allow a Communist dictator to commit aggression and genocide in the heart of Europe. Those are the lessons. Those acts assault our values. America is more than a piece of real estate. America is a series of moral principles that begin with the right to life and liberty that the Declaration says our creator gave us."

Environment

New Democrats believe in using performance-based, market-oriented, and civic-minded strategies to drive continuous and efficient improvement in environmental quality.

Lieberman serves on the Environment Committee, where recent activities include the protection of barrier islands and groundwater resources, investigation of the environmental effects of bioengineering, review of new technologies and scientific standards in achieving infrastructural growth and natural habitat renewal, and oversight of the Superfund program, solid waste and recycled materials, stratospheric ozone depletion, global climate change, private property rights, and federal regulatory reform.

Lieberman also serves on two subcommittees: Clean Air, Wetlands, Private Property, and Nuclear Safety; and Transportation and Infrastructure.

Lieberman has worked to strengthen clean air standards, and played a key role in winning passage of the landmark Clean Air Act Amendments in 1990. Early in his Senate career, he wrote a letter to the editor of the *Washington Post* (6/18/89) that could be presented as a textbook example of the New Democrat approach as applied to the environment.

Lieberman's letter responded to an earlier column by a former Reagan official that stressed the cost of the proposed legislation. The writer had minimized the health effects of air pollution, describing them as "transitory and self-limiting." Lieberman marshals testimony of medical experts on the effects of ozone, which "can kill lung cells, interfere with the lungs' self-cleaning mechanisms, decrease the lungs' ability to kill viruses and bacteria and impair the immune system."

Lieberman also pointed out the hidden costs of disease associated with high levels of ozone and other pollutants. He also specified the cost of the proposed changes to automobile standards: $140, compared with $220 for a power-window option.

Lieberman's letter concluded:

"Confronted by the severe health risks posed by urban smog, we cannot afford to disregard truly cost-effective methods of control. 'Clean air isn't free,' as [the Op-Ed writer] points out. But the public is tired of paying the price of dirty air, and is willing to do its part to clean it up."

In New Democrat fashion, Lieberman doesn't dismiss the issue of cost, and he also stresses the truism that "you get what you pay for."

In a *Washington Post* article (11/4/91) Lieberman argues: "We cannot drill our way out [of dependence on foreign oil]. The only way to bring our country into the 21st century and beyond is to develop a constructive energy policy that reduces our dependence on oil. We must emphasize energy efficiency, conservation and the development of renewable and alternative fuels."

Lieberman supports new ways of leveraging government involvement akin to the innovative DOD approaches. Along with Senator Max Baucus (D-Mont.) and Senator Barbara Mikulski (D-Md.), he sponsored 1993's National Environmental Technology Act. This act would have pushed government agencies to adopt and foster new technologies and also would have created a new department within the EPA. The National Environmental Technologies Institute (NETI) would have used government funding to form partnerships with private business to develop commercially viable remediation and pollution prevention methods.

In 1997, in the midst of the NAFTA debates, Lieberman wrote an editorial in the *Chrisitan Science Monitor* (4/24/97), making a strong case for international cooperation in developing effective approaches to dealing with global warming:

"If we don't set long-term greenhouse emissions limits now, and instead wait to see just how our climate changes, it may be too late when we do act. Greenhouse gases remain in the atmosphere for decades—even centuries—before leaving the atmosphere, so we need to begin reductions soon to achieve a useful long-term effect. A new generation of energy-efficient technologies requires a long lead time for development and implementation.

"As we enter full-scale international negotiations this year, I hope we will take a hard look at climate changes already occurring here, and the implications for our future if they continue and grow. If nations of the world fail to act in concert in the face of hard facts, consequences for humankind will be enormous. There are no benefits from delay."

He also wrote legislation to hold oil and shipping companies liable for the damage they cause; he helped co-author the Pollution Prosecution Act of 1990, which quadrupled the number of EPA investigators; and he was an early supporter of brownfields legislation.

Closer to home, Lieberman worked to create Connecticut's first national park at (Weir Farm), promoted a national wildlife refuge along the Connecticut River, and passed legislation to establish an EPA office in Connecticut dedicated to cleaning up the Long Island Sound.

Health Care

New Democrats want to create an Information Age health care system in which every American has the resources to purchase private health insurance in a marketplace where health plans and providers compete on the basis of both quality and cost.

Lieberman was an early opponent of the Clinton health care plan and voted against it. Just before the 1994 midterm elections, Lieberman described the plan as "a top-down, big-welfare-state kind of program," an initiative that set back New Democrat efforts to reshape the party.

In his Senate terms, Lieberman has worked with members of both parties to improve access and quality in our health care system. He co-sponsored the Kennedy-Kassebaum bill to allow people to change jobs without risking the loss of their health insurance. He is now fighting to provide patients with reliable "report cards" assessing doctors and hospitals, so consumers can make more informed judgments and get the best care available. And Lieberman has worked hard to reach consensus on a real Patients Bill of Rights to return decision-making authority to doctors and patients.

Media Content

New Democrats believe government should promote tools for helping parents control their kids' exposure to media violence and sex.

This has become one of Lieberman's signature issues, and it's one he feels most strongly about. In an interview with *Variety* in 1997, he says he first became aware of the problem when he discovered his then-four-year-old daughter watching "Married with Children."

In his first Senate term, Lieberman began his campaign for labeling of video games marketed to children. In a *USA Today* editorial debate (12/6/93), Lieberman wrote:

"If we can require the hardware company to put a label on a stepladder warning us about the top step, can't we require the video-game company to warn us about the decapitations or sexual violence its game depicts? If we're labeling products that can harm our kids' bodies, we should be able to label products that can harm our kids' minds."

Later that year, during a Senate committee hearing, Lieberman singled out Sega's Night Trap game, which features brutal crimes including murder. The game also includes footage of live actresses in skimpy clothing. Sega spokesman Bill White said: "Games aren't just for kids anymore." Lieberman replied: "It simply should be off the market."

His battle continued into his second term.

In 1995, Lieberman and Senator Sam Nunn (D-Ga.) teamed up with William Bennett's Empower America organization to single out advertisers on daytime "trash TV." The organization targeted sponsors of controversial and confrontational talk shows such as Jenny Jones, Sally Jesse Raphael, Jerry Springer, Montel Williams, Maury Povich, Geraldo, Charles Perez, Rolonda, Ricki Lake, and Richard Bey.

Broadcasting & Cable magazine (12/11/95) reported that "There is evidence that the efforts already have had an impact. Since October, Procter & Gamble, Kraft, and Sears, Roebuck & Co have announced they will no longer advertise on shows targeted by Empower America."

While some stations refused to run the ads, the magazine also reported positive response from broadcasters and advertising professionals:

" 'It's great. Syndicators and TV operators all have to think about what is on the air,' said Philip Jones, president, Meredith Corp. Broadcasting group. . . . 'I don't see a damn thing wrong with it.' . . .

"The campaign against sleaze also was embraced in at least some offices along Madison Avenue. 'Even though [the shows] generate good ratings, advertisers want an environment that reflects well on their product,' says H. Nass, of Foote, Cone & Belding. The sensational programs targeted by Bennett, Nunn and Lieberman have been losing their luster over the last six months, says Nass. During the same period, advertising rates on the shows have declined approximately 10%."

Lieberman continued his efforts throughout 1996, continuing to work with Bennett and C. Delores Tucker, chairwoman of the National Political Congress of Black Women. *Insight on the News* (2/3/97) called the group "the Mod Squad of family-values programming" and named the three "winners" in the ongoing battle. Lieberman also worked with Texas Republican Rep. Lamar Smith to call for a "family-friendly" evening time slot on broadcast and cable television.

In an article in *Broadcasting & Cable* magazine (5/19/97), Lieberman assessed the upcoming fall season from one of the networks: "NBC seems to run a close second to Fox on the raunch meter and has made its content worse." He accused the network of "[putting] profits ahead of what's best for the country."

Lieberman was the Congressional sponsor of the so-called V-Chip law which offers parents more direct control of television viewing by their young children, and also helped write legislation calling on the Federal Trade Commission to investigate the entertainment industry's marketing efforts, targeting children in promoting violent movies and games.

Last year (5/17/99), Lieberman spoke to *Broadcast & Cable* magazine, outlining his views on the subject:

"I'd like to see the media self-control, self-regulate. I'd like to see the media decide that they ought to all adopt codes of conduct in which they agree that they are not going to compete downward. . . .

"I don't want to get into a lot of governmental regulations. I don't want to start having the government decide what's acceptable and what's not acceptable. But there's such a rising chorus of anxiety in our country and anger about this that I'm afraid people will begin to move toward more intervention in the entertainment marketplace than is really wanted."

Education

New Democrats support efforts to improve public education through high common standards, choice and competition, accountability for results, and the resources needed to achieve them.

Lieberman supports both school vouchers and charter schools, policies many Democrats oppose. The Low Income School Choice Demonstration bill, co-sponsored by Leiberman, would have set up a pilot project for federally financed vouchers to be distributed to low-income families. The vouchers could then be used to pay for tuition at any private school in the district. The magazine *The Christian Century* (4/19/95) reported the response to the bill:

"The Coats-Lieberman proposal immediately drew

fire from the Washington-based Americans United for the Separation of Church and State. 'Public funds may not be used for private religious purposes,' said Barry Lynn, executive director of Americans United. 'No tax dollars may be directed into the coffers of private religious schools.'

"But Richard Cizik, policy analyst in the Washington office of the National Association of Evangelicals, welcomed the Coats-Lieberman bill as reflecting a decade-old NAE position. 'Our opinion is that this [voucher system] is the way to go with education, health and welfare benefits,' Cizik said. He pointed to the use of vouchers in the current federal child care program allowing recipients to use their vouchers for religiously based child care providers.

"But Lynn took issue with the comparison. 'Religious instruction must be paid for only through voluntary contributions of church members,' he maintained. 'Forcing taxpayers to support schools through a voucher system is nothing less than a religion tax.' "

(Lynn needn't have worried about this particular measure. The bill was read twice and referred to the Committee on Labor and Human Resources, from which it has not emerged.)

Lieberman also has proposed landmark education reform legislation that would dramatically increase funding for disadvantaged students, give states and local districts greater autonomy in targeting their resources, and set tough accountability standards to demand results.

Campaign Finance Reform

It is perhaps telling that a search of the Democratic Leadership Council website shows only six documents containing the phrase "campaign finance reform" and only one document devoted entirely to the issue.

In July 1997, Lieberman and Republican Sen. Fred Thompson presided over Senate Governmental Affairs Committee hearings into campaign financing for the 1996 election. Observers singled out Lieberman's calm, reasonable, even-handed approach to the investigation. During the hearings, Lieberman supported Thompson's assessment that China may well have used campaign donations to influence the 1996 race. This stance flew in the face of Democrat and media response, which had dismissed Thompson's accusation.

Watching his performance, Arianna Huffington wrote in the *Washington Times*:

"At a time when Attorney General Janet Reno refuses to appoint a special counsel to investigate fund-raising abuses, when House Majority Leader Dick Armey looks Americans in the eye and denies his undeniable involvement in the coup against the speaker, when Vice President Al Gore claims that an event at a cash-filled temple was not a fund-raiser and when former Republican National Committee Chairman Haley Barbour insists the National Policy Forum was anything other than a front for raising soft money, Sen. Joe Lieberman of Connecticut seems cut from a different cloth."

A *New York Times* editorial stated:

"The Senate hearings into last year's campaign fundraising abuses were destined to make every professional politician squirm. In the last three weeks, Democratic and Republican senators have alternated between distrust and defensiveness as they rummaged for embarrassing disclosures in each other's political closets. Little by little, however, the proceedings led by Senator Fred Thompson are fulfilling their mandate to uncover the abuses of last year and lay the foundation for reform. This is largely attributable to Mr. Thompson and the one Democrat who has tried hardest to rise above partisanship, Senator Joseph Lieberman of Connecticut. . . .

"Alone among the Democrats, Mr. Lieberman has tried not to dismiss the sleaze around his own party's fund-raising operations."

A subsequent *New York Times* article (7/29/97) pointed out the senator's low-key approach: "Lieberman speaks less colorfully than colleagues like Democrat Robert G. Torricelli, of New Jersey, who last week dramatically invoked the spirit of Mario Cuomo and others whose political careers, he suggested, were the victims of improper Republican campaign contributions.

"Mr. Lieberman often asks basic questions: Why would someone who is not an American citizen and has no major interests here contribute huge sums to be involved in our political process?"

After the hearings, Lieberman wrote the first major campaign finance law to pass in a generation, which closed a loophole that allowed political organizations to raise and spend money in secret.

Lieberman also has used his position on the Government Affairs Committee to expose government waste, such as the federal contracts that paid $69 an hour for security guards, and the highway noise barrier projects that were built along stretches of road where nobody lived to hear the noise. Lieberman played a key role in winning passage of the Congressional Accountability Act, which makes Congress live by the same laws it applies to the nation.

Sex in the Workplace Part I

On October 12, 1991, TV viewers who tuned in expecting the usual Saturday-morning cartoons saw something better scripted for Theater of the Absurd: Senator Orrin Hatch reading aloud from *The Exorcist*. Senator Hatch's performance was only one of many strange and unsettling moments of the Clarence Thomas hearings.

At the time, Thomas was a federal judicial court judge in Washington, D.C.; he'd succeeded Robert Bork in the position. Thomas was a graduate of Yale Law School, a strongly conservative thinker, and an African-American from a poor southern background. After George Bush nominated Thomas to replace the retiring Thurgood Marshall, attention was focused on Thomas's views, such as opposition to affirmative action and abortion. Others questioned whether Thomas's relatively limited judicial experience qualified him for the highest court. Another point of contention was his belief in the principles of natural law, defined as "a body of law or a specific principle of law that is held to be derived from nature and binding upon human society in the absence of or in addition to positive law," such as statute law. Natural law was an important influence on the writing of Thomas Jefferson and his contemporaries; it's often appealed to by those who look for the original intent of the authors of the Constitution.

As pundits from all points on the political spectrum sifted through Thomas's judicial record, a strongly partisan standoff developed.

In an article for *The New Republic* (9/9/91), Jeff Rosen summarized the liberal response to the nomination:

"As Clarence Thomas prepares to face the Senate, liberals are continuing to portray him as a bizarre, unpredictable, conservative activist—a justice who might strike down child labor laws, subvert the civil liberties of all but the unborn, and banish women from the workplace because the Creator commands them to be wives and mothers. Kate Michelman of the National Abortion Rights Action League calls Thomas's writings 'very devastating, and shocking . . . a smoking gun.' Laurence Tribe of Harvard suggests that Thomas's views about natural law threaten 'the fate of self-government in the U.S.' Erwin Chemerinsky of People for the American Way warns that Thomas has 'openly allied himself with [Robert] Bork's philosophy.' And the NAACP has concluded that 'Judge Thomas's conservatism generally favors a government's interest over an individual's.' "

From a conservative point of view, the liberal furor could be explained by looking at the left's own positions. In a piece for *The National Review* (8/12/91), William McGurn quotes an unnamed Bush administration official: "Clarence is a hand grenade spinning around in the Democrats' living room. His nomination touches all their key constituencies: Jews on quotas, Catholics on religion, blacks on civil rights. If I'm a Democratic senator, right now I have to be asking myself, 'Do I really want to pick this thing up?' "

McGurn goes on to assess Thomas's record as head of the Equal Opportunity Commission during the Reagan administration, as well as his legal decisions and writings as federal jurist. McGurn quotes a Reagan Justice Department official's assessment of the nominee:

"Thurgood Marshall was a great advocate and a great symbol. That can't—and shouldn't—be taken away from him. But as a jurist he did not author a single major civil-rights case. With Clarence Thomas we may get a real intellectual contribution to the course of law."

What followed was anything but an intellectual contribution to law. The morning of October 6, a National Public Radio story and an article in *New York Newsday* revealed allegations leveled at Thomas by Anita Hill, a law professor at the University of Oklahoma and Thomas's former employee at the Equal Opportunity Commission. According to Hill, Thomas had sexually harassed her, engaging in lewd conversation about subjects including pubic hair and porn stars. Hill had come forward on September 23, believing her statement would be kept confidential. It wasn't.

The heated partisan rhetoric became white-hot. The judicial issues were largely set aside. For the rest of 1991, the press was full of stories on sexual harassment, erotomania, and related issues.

The Senate Judiciary Committee postponed their hearing on Thomas's nomination so Hill's charges could be heard. Because of overwhelming public interest, the committee also decided to televise the hearings.

At this point, Lieberman supported Thomas's nomination, one of thirteen Democrats who crossed party lines to do so. Lieberman had remained fairly neutral in the ongoing debate; in a *WP* article after the hearings, Lieberman said, "I wouldn't have nominated him. But there wasn't enough reason not to vote for him."

However, as Anita Hill's allegations were explored in the hearings, Lieberman's support weakened. There was no single "ah-ha!" moment, no flash of clarity or insight into who was telling the truth. Instead, as he describes in the article, Lieberman had to assess new information with no certainty of truth on either side. In the *Washington Post* article, Lieberman summed up his thoughts at this point: "Are my doubts serious enough? I don't want to send someone to the Supreme Court who is guilty of sexual harassment. On the other hand, I don't want to be unfair to him."

The issue transcended politics and became a matter

of governance. In keeping with his policy of forgoing Sabbath prohibitions for the sake of important governmental duties, Lieberman and his wife spent that Friday evening watching the televised hearings.

As he continued to watch the hearings, Lieberman became more disturbed. Still, a clear answer evaded him. As described in the *Wall Street Journal* article, he "awakened suddenly on the day of the confirmation vote. In his morning prayer, he 'asked for good judgment.' "

With Thomas's confirmation in danger, Republicans were pushing hard for support. That morning, as he and an aide drove to the Capitol, Lieberman got a call from President Bush. The president argued that the case against Thomas hadn't been persuasive; Lieberman told Bush he still hadn't made up his mind.

Throughout the day, Lieberman continued to weigh the testimony, discussing the matter with colleagues, reporters, and his wife. Finally, he made his decision: to vote against confirmation. As he recalled later, "You really just have to decide what you think is right. . . . This was the toughest decision I've made since I've been here. I voted with a profound sense of humility and a prayer that I did the right thing."

In Lieberman's second term, he would face another tough decision, one that again dealt with matters of conscience, morality, sexual misbehavior. Americans would once again be amazed, and appalled, by the topics of everyday conversation in the halls and offices of government.

5

Sex and the White House

Joseph Lieberman first met Bill Clinton in 1970. Clinton, a student at Yale Law School, volunteered for Lieberman's first campaign for a Connecticut House seat, knocking on doors and handing out flyers in New Haven.

As the political careers of both men developed, they continued to be friendly colleagues. When the Democratic Leadership Council was formed, Arkansas governor Bill Clinton was one of the first politicians to join. In 1990, shortly after Lieberman joined the Senate and became active in the DLC, Clinton became the organization's president. The two men worked closely as they helped develop the ideas behind the New Democrat. Lieberman was the first northern senator to endorse the Clinton candidacy in 1992.

As one of Clinton's trusted informal advisors, Lieberman often had to field late-night phone calls during which the president immediately would plunge into detailed discussion of policy or strategy. In his book *The Choice*, Bob Woodward described Lieberman's reaction: "It was like being a fireman or worse. With a Clinton call, Lieberman had to be able to go from a deep sleep to the full alert of high-intensity intellectual conversation in a few seconds."

Lieberman and other DLC stalwarts strongly disagreed with Clinton's first major policy initiative, the health care plan, which many believe helped usher in the Republican Revolt of 1994. Woodward describes Clinton's state of mind after the bitter public debate and the plan's lopsided defeat, followed by the Republican triumph in Congressional elections. The president felt that the public's perception of Democratic policy had been inaccurate; he was frustrated trying to operate as the head of a diverse and contentious party and simultaneously put forward the changes he longed to make. Woodward quotes Lieberman's response:

" 'You know,' Lieberman said in the wise, optimistic tone of a rabbi, 'people haven't given up on you. Some people love you, some people hate you. And there's this group in the middle, which is probably still the majority, that is open to hearing you out. This thing can flip back as dramatically by 1996 as it did in 1994.' "

By August 1998, very few Americans remained in that "group in the middle."

Special Prosecutor Kenneth Starr originally was appointed to investigate alleged financial fraud in Bill and Hillary Clintons' Whitewater real estate investment. The investigation extended to several other suspected "-gates," all of which were duly reported by the media, to the general indifference of most Americans. But Starr's investigation would soon enter areas far more exciting than anything that had come before.

In late 1997, Starr's team began focusing on rumors that Clinton had engaged in an extramarital affair with a young White House intern. This affair had, in turn, led to perjury and obstruction of justice in Paula Jones's civil lawsuit against Clinton for sexual harassment. What had been inside-the-Beltway gossip became public in January 1998. Later that month, at a White House event, Clinton addressed the rumors directly. He told reporters: "I did not have a relationship with that woman, Miss Lewinsky." The next day, Starr opened a formal grand jury investigation of Lewinsky's claims.

For the next few months, investigation continued and expanded, as did the media coverage. The criticism and ridicule of the president grew harsher as did the responses from Clinton's team. The impassioned and highly polarized debate—He's lying! She's crazy!—recalled the public response to the Clarence Thomas hearings.

While Clinton's defenders remained unequivocal in public, they were growing more and more concerned. Publicly and privately, the president continued to insist that there was absolutely no truth to the allegations. None. The president's trusted friends and colleagues continued to face the media barrage and defend Clinton vigorously.

In early August 1998, a decisive point was reached. "That woman" gave Starr a navy-blue dress stained with, she said, the president's semen. The prosecutor promptly sent the dress to the FBI for DNA analysis. Unlike the Thomas-Hill debate, this "Did he or didn't he?" question would be definitively answered.

The president did not wait for the results of the FBI's tests. On August 17, he called a press conference in which he admitted to a relationship with Ms. Lewinsky that was "wrong" and "not appropriate."

If he expected his admission would end the scandal,

he was wrong. *U.S. News and World Report* gathered a sampling of editorial response across the nation:

Anchorage Times:
   "Clinton has thrown himself into the trash heap of history. And the nation has reason to mourn the shame he has brought to his office."

San Jose (Cal.) *Mercury-News:*
   "[Clinton] should be profoundly ashamed, and the shame should haunt him for the rest of his life."

Paul Greenberg, columnist, *Arkansas Democrat-Gazette*:
   "Most of the folks who cover Bill Clinton eventually reach a moment of truth.
   "There comes a time—it's usually definite and memorable—when they stop giving him the benefit of the mounting doubt, when they just give up on him and vow that they'll never be suckered again. The difference between a Clinton critic and a Clinton apologist is that the apologist hasn't had his moment of truth yet."

Modesto (Cal.) *Bee:*
   "A new low in national discourse."

Columbia (S.C.) *State:*
   "He lied to us—not inadvertently, not as a momentary lapse, but deliberately, insistently and over a long period of time. He should resign."

St. Louis Post-Dispatch:
   "Trust is the glue that binds a leader to the people in a democracy. Mr. Clinton has lost that trust."

New York Times:

"Here was a man of compassionate impulse and lofty ambition who went to Washington with virtually every imaginable political skill except one. He seemed to think he was immune from a rule that leaps out from any reading of modern presidencies. Everything comes out sooner or later."

Denver Post:

"The most honorable course remaining is resignation. After all the other rubbish is cleared away, credibility and integrity are at the ethical core of this fiasco, and the president doesn't have them. Out of respect for the office, he should step down."

Post-Tribune (northwest Ind.):

"The president put the country through an unnecessary tabloid hell that left parents trying to explain to their children what oral sex was, what the notorious stain was and, worse, why it was OK for the president to lie and not them."

Chattanooga (Tn.) *Times:*

"Whatever good things Mr. Clinton has accomplished during his presidency will be forever tainted by the brazen recklessness that has undermined the legacy he hoped to leave the nation."

St. Petersburg Times:

"President Clinton, who habitually has lied about everything from marijuana to his golf score, has been caught in his biggest and broadest lie yet. How can he possibly provide leadership on Social Security, or race relations, or—God forbid—war?"

E.J. Dionne, columnist, *Washington Post:*

"Clinton is right about one thing: This has to end. A substantial majority of Americans would prefer that this matter go away and that Clinton serve out his term. But they'd also like to be able to trust him. At the moment, many who feel him no ill will don't think they can. He owes the nation, and his supporters especially, more than he's given so far."

Orlando (Fl.) *Sentinel:*

"Enough is enough. If Mr. Clinton is an honorable man, he will resign and let the country move on."

Republicans soon took up the call for Clinton to resign. A *Washington Post* article (8/28/98) reported: "At a time when most Republican political leaders are keeping a cautious distance from the controversy enveloping President Clinton, House Majority Whip Tom DeLay has launched a campaign that he hopes will put pressure on the president to resign." DeLay said the censure proposed by Democrats was inadequate. His colleagues quoted in the story agreed:

"Rep. Barbara Cubin (R-Wyo.) said the president should step aside because he had lied under oath, adding that she believed other Republican members shared her views.

" 'I think people are reluctant to say it, for one reason or another, but ultimately when we speak to one another, I think that's what most folks believe,' Cubin said. . . .

"Rep. Thomas J. Bliley Jr. (R-Va.) yesterday joined the chorus. 'We've had several very talented officers in the military that were involved in scandal and they resigned. . . . There's no question he's brought disrespect to the office, and he's got to correct it.' "

The Clinton loyalists seemed to be paralyzed. Several were quoted in a *Los Angeles Times* (8/18/98) article:

"White House Press Secretary Mike McCurry said his feelings were 'predictable,' but added, 'I'm not going to comment on them.' McCurry had been the only White House staffer to publicly speculate that [President] Clinton had no 'simple, innocent explanation' because, he told the *Chicago Tribune*, 'I think we would have offered that up already.'

"A somber Lanny J. Davis, who supported Clinton on television more than 70 times since he left his White House position as special counsel on Jan. 30, declined to discuss whether he was disappointed that Clinton had not been entirely up front about the nature of his dealings with Lewinsky.

" 'Whatever feelings I have I will only share with him and Mrs. Clinton,' he said.

"Davis, now an attorney in private practice, said he stood up publicly for the President 'as a longtime friend of the Clintons, as a lawyer and most important, as someone who still believes in the Clinton presidency and what he's done for the country.

" 'I don't regret standing by him for those three reasons, especially the third one,' Davis said.

"Political consultant James Carville, another ardent Clinton defender, said on CNN's 'Larry King Live' that 'I don't feel betrayed. He has my undying loyalty. I think he's been a great President and he's been a great friend. . . . I feel fine.' And he kept on spinning: 'I would paraphrase Dante. The hot blooded will be judged easier than the cold blooded.'

"But on the same program, former Press Secretary Dee Dee Myers described herself as 'less willing to forgive . . . at the moment.' She noted that Clinton "sent

[supporters] out there, put their credibility at risk, cost a
lot of innocent people a lot of time and a lot of money
[in defending themselves]."

Focused on spin and political positioning, no one
from the Democratic side of the aisle delivered a statement of blunt, unequivocal criticism. Until September 3.

That day, Senator Lieberman took the Senate floor.
He began by saying, "Mr. President, I rise today to make
the most difficult statement I've made on this floor in the
10 years I've been a member of the United States Senate." What followed was the kind of morality-based criticism that, up to this point, had been heard only from
Republicans. The complete text of Lieberman's speech
follows.

Senator Joseph Lieberman's September 3, 1998, Speech to the U.S. Senate

Mr. President, I rise today to make a most difficult
and distasteful statement. For me, probably the most
difficult statement I've made on this floor in the 10
years I've been a member of the United States Senate.

On August 17th, President Clinton testified before
a grand jury convened by the independent counsel, and
then talked to the American people about his relationship with Monica Lewinsky, a former White House intern. He told us that the relationship was, quote, "not
appropriate," that it was, quote, "wrong," and that it
was, quote, "a critical lapse of judgment," and "a personal failure" on his part.

In addition, after seven months of denying that he
had engaged in a sexual relationship with Ms. Lewinsky, the president admitted that his, quote, "public
comments about this matter gave a false impression."
He said, "I misled people."

Mr. President, my immediate reaction to this statement that night it was delivered was deep disappointment and personal anger. I was disappointed because the president of the United States had just confessed to engaging in an extramarital affair with a young woman in his employ and to willfully deceiving the nation about his conduct. I was personally angry because President Clinton had, by his disgraceful behavior, jeopardized his administration's historic record of accomplishment, much of which grew out of the principles and programs that he and I and many others had worked on together in the New Democratic movement.

I was also angry because I was one of the many people who had said over the preceding seven months that if the president clearly and explicitly denies the allegations against him, then of course I believe him.

Well, since that Monday night, I have not commented on this matter publicly. I thought I had an obligation to consider the president's admissions more objectively, less personally, and to try to put them in a clearer perspective. And I felt that I owed that much to the president for whom I have great affection and admiration and who I truly believed has worked tirelessly to make life tangibly better in so many ways for so many Americans.

But the truth is that after much reflection, my feelings of disappointment and anger have not dissipated, except now these feelings have gone beyond my personal dismay to a larger, graver sense of loss for our country, a reckoning of the damage that the president's conduct has done to the proud legacy of his presidency and ultimately an accounting of the impact of his actions on our democracy and its moral foundations.

The implications for our country are so serious that I feel a responsibility to my constituents in Connecticut

as well as to my conscience to voice my concerns forth-
rightly and publicly, and I can think of no more appropriate place to do that than on this great Senate floor.

I've chosen to speak particularly at this time before
the independent counsel files his report because while
we do not know enough yet to answer the question of
whether there are legal consequences of the president's
conduct, we do know enough from what the president
acknowledged on August 17th to answer a separate and
distinct set of questions about the moral consequences
for our country.

Mr. President, I have come to this floor many times
in the past to speak with my colleagues about the concerns which are so widely shared in this chamber and
throughout the nation that our society's standards are
sinking, that our common moral code is deteriorating,
and that our public life in coarsening. In doing so, I
have specifically criticized leaders of the entertainment
industry for the way they have used the enormous influence they wield to weaken our common values.

And now, because the president commands at least
as much attention and exerts at least as much influence
on our collective consciousness as any Hollywood ce-
lebrity or television show, it is hard to ignore the impact of the misconduct the president has admitted to on
our culture, on our character and on our children.

To begin with, I must respectfully disagree with the
president's contention that his relationship with Monica Lewinsky and the way in which he misled us about
it is nobody's business but his family's, and that "even
presidents have private lives," as he said. Whether he
or we think it fair or not, the reality is in 1998 that a
president's private life is public. Contemporary news
media standards will have it no other way. And surely
this president was given fair notice of that by the

amount of time the news media has dedicated to investigating his personal life during the 1992 campaign and in the years since.

But there is more to this than modern media intrusiveness. The president is not just the elected leader of our country. He is, as presidential scholar Clinton Rossetter observed, and I quote, "the one-man distillation of the American people," and as President Taft said at another time, "the personal embodiment and representative of their dignity and majesty."

So when his personal conduct is embarrassing, it is sadly so not just for him and his family. It is embarrassing for all of us as Americans. The president is a role model who, because of his prominence and the moral authority that emanates from his office, sets standards of behavior for the people he serves.

His duty, as the Reverend Nathan Baxter of the National Cathedral here in Washington said in a recent sermon, is nothing less than the stewardship of our values. So no matter how much the president or others may wish to compartmentalize the different spheres of his life, the inescapable truth is that the president's private conduct can and often does have profound public consequences.

In this case, the president apparently had extramarital relations with an employee half his age and did so in the workplace, in the vicinity of the Oval Office. Such behavior is not just inappropriate. It is immoral. And it is harmful, for it sends a message of what is acceptable behavior to the larger American family, particularly to our children, which is as influential as the negative messages communicated by the entertainment culture.

If you doubt that, just ask America's parents about the intimate and frequently unseemly sexual questions their young children have been asking them and discussing since the president's relationship with Ms. Lewinsky became public seven months ago. I have had many of those conversations with parents, particularly in Connecticut. And from them I conclude that parents across our country feel, much as I do, that something very sad and sordid has happened in American life when I cannot watch the news on television with my 10-year-old daughter anymore.

This unfortunately is all-too-familiar territory for America's families in today's anything-goes culture, where sexual promiscuity is treated as just another lifestyle choice with little risk of adverse consequences. It is this mindset that has helped to threaten the stability and integrity of the family, which continues to be the most important unit of civilized society, the place where we raise our children and teach them to be responsible citizens, to develop and nurture their personal and moral faculties.

President Clinton, in fact, has shown during the course of his presidency that he understands this and the broad concern in the public about the threat to the family. He has used the bully pulpit of his presidency to eloquently and effectively call for the renewal of our common values, particularly the principle of personal responsibility and our common commitment to family. And he has spoken out admirably against sexual promiscuity among teenagers in clear terms of right and wrong, emphasizing the consequences involved.

Now, all of that makes the president's misconduct so confusing and so damaging. The president's relationship with Ms. Lewinsky not only contradicted the values he has publicly embraced over the last six years. It has, I fear, compromised his moral authority at a time when Americans of every political persuasion agree that the decline of the family is one of the most pressing problems we are facing.

Nevertheless, I believe that the president could have lessened the harm his relationship with Ms. Lewinsky has caused if he had acknowledged his mistake and spoken with candor about it to the American people shortly after it became public in January. But, as we now know, he chose not to do this.

This deception is particularly troubling because it was not just a reflexive and, in many ways, understandable human act of concealment to protect himself and his family from what he called the embarrassment of his own conduct when he was confronted with it in the deposition in the Jones case, but rather it was the intentional and premeditated decision to do so.

In choosing this path, I fear that the president has undercut the efforts of millions of American parents who are naturally trying to instill in our children the value of honesty. As most any mother and father knows, kids have a singular ability to detect double standards.

So we can safely assume that it will be that much more difficult to convince our sons and daughters of the importance of telling the truth when the most powerful man in the nation evades it. Many parents I have spoken with in Connecticut confirm this unfortunate consequence.

The president's intentional and consistent statements, more deeply, may also undercut the trust that the American people have in his word. Under the Constitution, as presidential scholar Richard Neustadt has noted, the president's ultimate source of authority, particularly his moral authority, is the power to persuade, to mobilize public opinion, to build consensus behind a common agenda. And at this, the president has been extraordinarily effective. But that power hinges on the president's support among the American public and their faith and confidence in his motivations and agenda, yes, but also in his word.

As Teddy Roosevelt once explained, "My power vanishes into thin air the instant that my fellow citizens, who are straight and honest, cease to believe that I represent them and fight for what is straight and honest. That is all the strength that I have," Roosevelt said.

Sadly, with his deception, President Clinton may have weakened the great power and strength that he possesses of which President Roosevelt spoke. I know this is a concern that many of my colleagues share, which is to say that the president has hurt his credibility and therefore perhaps his chances of moving his policy agenda forward.

But I believe that the harm the president's actions have caused extends beyond the political arena. I am afraid that the misconduct the president has admitted may be reinforcing one of the worst messages being delivered by our popular culture, which is that values are fungible. And I am concerned that his misconduct may help to blur some of the most important bright lines of right and wrong in our society.

Mr. President, I said at the outset that this was a very difficult statement to write and deliver. That is true, very true. And it is true in large part because it is so personal and yet needs to be public, but also because of my fear that it will appear unnecessarily judgmental. I truly regret this. I know from the Bible that only God can judge people. The most that we can do is to comment without condemning individuals. And in this case, I have tried to comment on the consequences of the president's conduct on our country.

I know that the president is far from alone in the

wrongdoing he has admitted. We as humans are all imperfect. We are all sinners. Many have betrayed a loved one and most have told lies. Members of Congress have certainly been guilty of such behavior, as have some previous presidents. We try to understand—we must try to understand the complexity and difficulty of personal relationships, which should give us pause before passing judgment on them. We all fall short of the standards our best values set for us. Certainly I do.

But the president, by virtue of the office he sought and was elected to, has traditionally been held to a higher standard. This is as it should be, because the American president, as I quoted earlier, is not just a one-man distillation of the American people but today the most powerful person in the world. And as such, the consequences of his misbehavior, even private misbehavior, are much greater than that of an average citizen, a CEO or even a senator.

That's what I believe presidential scholar James David Barber, in his book *The Presidential Character,* was getting at when he wrote that the public demands, quote, "a sense of legitimacy from and in the presidency. There is more to this than dignity, more than propriety. The president is expected to personify our betterness in an inspiring way, to express in what he does and is, not just what he says, a moral idealism which, in much of the public mind, is the very opposite of politics," end quote, just as the American people are demanding of their leaders, though they are also fundamentally fair and forgiving, which is why I was so hopeful the president could begin to repair the damage done with his address to the nation on the 17th.

But, like so many others, I came away feeling that, for reasons that are thoroughly human, he missed a great opportunity that night. He failed to clearly articulate to the American people that he recognized how significant and consequential his wrongdoing was and how badly he felt about it. He failed to show, I think, that he understood his behavior had diminished the office he holds and the country he serves and that it is inconsistent with the mainstream American values that he has advanced as president.

And I regret that he failed to acknowledge that while Mr. Starr and Ms. Lewinsky, Mrs. Tripp and the news media have each, in their own way, contributed to the crisis we now face, his presidency would not be imperiled if it had not been for the behavior he himself described as wrong and inappropriate.

Because the conduct the president admitted to that night was serious and his assumption of responsibility inadequate, the last three weeks have been dominated by a cacophony of media and political voices calling for impeachment or resignation or censure, while a lesser chorus implores us to move on and get this matter behind us.

Appealing as that latter option may be to many people who are understandably weary of this crisis, the transgressions the president has admitted to are too consequential for us to walk away and leave the impression for our children today and for our posterity tomorrow that what he acknowledges he did within the White House is acceptable behavior for our nation's leader. On the contrary, as I have said, it is wrong and unacceptable, and should be followed by some measure of public rebuke and accountability.

We in Congress, elected representatives of all the American people, are surely capable institutionally of expressing such disapproval through a resolution of reprimand or censure of the president for his misconduct. But it is premature to do so, as my colleagues of both parties seem to agree, until we have received the report of the independent counsel and the White House's response to it.

In the same way, it seems to me that talk of impeachment and resignation at this time is unjust and unwise. It is unjust because we do not know enough in fact, and will not until the independent counsel reports and the White House responds, to conclude whether we have crossed the high threshold our Constitution rightly sets for overturning the results of a popular election in our democracy and bringing on the national trauma of removing an incumbent president from office.

For now, in fact, all we know for certain is what the president acknowledged on August 17th. As far as I can see, the rest is rumor, speculation or hearsay, much less than is required by members of the House and Senate in the dispatch of the solemn responsibilities that the Constitution gives us in such circumstances.

And I believe that talk of impeachment and resignation now is unwise because it ignores the reality that while the independent counsel proceeds with his investigation, the president is still our nation's leader, our commander-in-chief. Economic uncertainty and other problems here at home, as well as the fiscal and political crises in Russia and Asia and the growing threats posed by Iraq, North Korea and worldwide terrorism, all demand the president's focused leadership.

For that reason, while the legal process moves forward, I believe it is important that we provide the president with the time and space and support he needs to carry out his most important duties and protect our national interest and security. That time and space may also give the president additional opportunities to accept personal responsibility for his behavior, to rebuild public trust in his leadership, to recommit himself to the values of opportunity, responsibility and community that brought him to office, and to act to heal the wounds in our national character.

In the meantime, as the debate on this matter proceeds and as the investigation goes forward, we would all be advised, I would respectfully suggest, to heed the wisdom of Abraham Lincoln's second annual address to Congress in 1862. With the nation at war with itself, President Lincoln warned, and I quote, "If there ever could be a time for mere catch arguments, that time is surely not now. In times like the present, men should utter nothing for which they would not willingly be responsible through time and eternity."

I believe that we are at such a time today. With so much at stake, we too must resist the impulse toward catch arguments and reflex reactions. Let us proceed in accordance with our nation's traditional moral compass, yes, but in a manner that is fair and at a pace that is deliberate and responsible.

Let us as a nation honestly confront the damage that the president's actions over the last seven months have caused, but not to the exclusion of the good that his leadership has done over the past six years, nor at the expense of our common interest as Americans. And let us be guided by the conscience of the Constitution, which calls on us to place the common good above any partisan or personal interest, as we now, in our time, work together to resolve this serious challenge to our democracy.

I thank the chair. I thank my colleagues. And I yield the floor.

Though some criticized Lieberman for stopping short of calling on the president to resign and others carped about his "moralizing" tone, the response was largely positive:

From the *New York Times* (9/4/99):

" 'It's good that a Democrat gave that speech . . . because everybody's going to try to use what [President] Clinton did to hold the Democrats down,' Mr. [Danny] Charleston said. 'I was wondering when Mr. Lieberman was going to speak up. He spoke for Connecticut.'

"From a working-class diner to the gabled grandeur of Yale University, most people interviewed here today said that for all the talk about Mr. Clinton's admission of an inappropriate relationship with Monica S. Lewinsky, Mr. Lieberman's measured condemnation of the President was about the most sensible thing they had heard on the topic."

From the *Chicago Tribune* (9/5/99):

"Sen. Joseph Lieberman, a Connecticut Democrat and a longtime political ally of President Clinton, delivered one of the most eloquent—and courageous—speeches the Senate has heard in many years, and one the country desperately needed to hear.

"Addressing the festering Clinton-Lewinsky scandal, Lieberman dared speak not just in terms of legality but also in terms of duty, honor and morality. And the result, for Clinton, was a denunciation more powerful than any legal indictment ever could be."

From the *Boston Globe* (9/5/99):

"Senator Joseph I. Lieberman, a Connecticut Democrat, performed several valuable services with his moving speech on the Senate floor focusing on what he called President Clinton's 'immoral' behavior.

"First, he stopped in its tracks the White House effort

to brush the scandal aside as if it had been resolved. Clinton's Aug. 17 admission of wrongdoing concluded by asking people to 'turn away' from talk of his personal behavior and 'return our attention to all the challenges and all the promise of the next American century.' The plea was hollow then; Lieberman rendered it inoperative."

From the St. Louis Post-Dispatch (9/6/99):

"In a few subdued minutes of eloquence on the Senate floor, Sen. Joseph I. Lieberman, D-Conn., provided more insight into the Clinton sex scandal than a dozen full-throated pundits on Sunday talk shows.

"The senator constructed a moral framework that Americans might use in evaluating the scandal. In that way Mr. Lieberman's speech was much more helpful than Minority Leader Richard A. Gephardt's on-again, off-again criticism of Mr. Clinton and Sen. John Ashcroft's hyper-partisan decision to hold hearings on whether a president can be indicted."

After Lieberman's speech, others from his party began to weigh in. As described in a *USA Today* article (9/8/98):

"Just as the White House feared, Sen. Joseph Lieberman's moral condemnation of President Clinton has brought a wave of agreement and even harsher criticism from other Democrats.

"The Connecticut Democrat's disappointment at Clinton's 'immorality' and deception, voiced on the Senate floor last week and echoed on national television over the weekend, appears to have expressed sentiment broadly held but until then unspoken among many in his own party.

"Two more Democratic senators chimed in within minutes, and more have followed in the days since."

Prodded on the issue by reporters, President Clinton said he agreed with Lieberman that his relationship with Monica Lewinsky was "indefensible" and then said he was "very sorry" about it.

An article in the *New York Times* (9/5/98) described Lieberman's reaction to Clinton's words:

"Mr. Lieberman said that he 'appreciated' Mr. Clinton's comments but thought that the President still needed to say more.

" 'As I saw him,' Mr. Lieberman said of watching Mr. Clinton on television this morning, 'I felt badly that he had to do it, but I knew he had to do it. This is a process. It's not a one-time thing. It's like having someone in your family with a problem. It doesn't end with a single statement. It's a process—of confrontation, repentance and reconstruction of the ties within the family.' "

In the August 7, 2000, *New Yorker,* the late English drama critic Kenneth Tynan describes in a diary a very bawdy and very brief tryst that took place between John Kennedy and Marlene Dietrich—in the White House. The president, according to this version of events, was particularly concerned to know whether his father, Joseph, had already slept with the German songstress before he did, and he was particularly pleased to learn from Ms. Dietrich that the older man had not done so.

Senator Lieberman, in making his broad condemnation of the President Clinton, had ignored such ironies and complexities from the American past. He'd also chosen to ignore the bitter political battle that had been waged by Republicans against the president ever since he'd appeared on the national scene in 1992—a battle that reached its culmination in the Lewinsky scandal. Never before had a chief executive been subjected to having his sex life investigated in exhausting depth and exhausting detail by a special prosecutor. Kenneth Starr spent roughly four years and $50 million looking for a charge, any charge, that would stick. It was an unprecedented attempt to distract and to humiliate—if not to unseat—a sitting president. And all the while, Clinton's political opposition, both in the media and in the Halls of Congress, took delight in the process. Yet nearly every poll taken during the scandal indicated that two-thirds of the general population did not feel that the president should lose his job over it. In fact, in some polls, his approval ratings rose. The Lewinsky affair was, the American public seemed to be saying, an adult matter and adult matters ventured into areas that had nothing to do with politics.

Rabbi Michael Lerner publishes *Tikkun* magazine in San Francisco. Tikkun is Hebrew for "to heal, to repair, and to transform the world," which was the mission of Lerner's periodical. Following Lieberman's nomination for vice-president, Lerner appeared on CNN on August 8, 2000, and was critical of the senator for defining morality too narrowly in terms of sexual conduct. Rabbi Lerner was one of the few commentators anywhere who questioned Lieberman's sweeping denunciation of the president.

"On social justice issues," he said, "Lieberman has not been very good. . . . He's weak in these areas and has moved the Democratic party away from its base. Sexual issues should not be the full measure of moral bankruptcy. Do not put ethics entirely in terms of sexual matters in private life. . . . Many see Lieberman as the Republicans' favorite Democrat."

It took another kind of courage to stand up during the Starr investigation and question the use of government power and funding to invade the private lives of others. It took a different kind of courage to demand an end to the hounding and the humiliation—a calling off of the dogs. It's hardly a coincidence that the most impassioned defense of the President came from Representatives Maxine Waters (CA), John Lewis (GA), and Barney Frank (MA), whose fierce loyalty reflected Clinton's years of devotion to issues important to minority groups including African Americans and gays.

It said something about Senator Lieberman that in September of 1998, he did not concern himself with past behaviors of American leaders but only with the present set of circumstances. This is not to suggest that he was merely being opportunistic in choosing to lambaste the president in such a public way. Rather, it may have been reflecting an idealism, and even a naiveté, that he'd managed to hold on to after several decades of political life. He could be accused of numerous things, but not cynicism, which may have been a tribute to his faith.

6

Al Gore's Historic Choice

Al Gore is nothing if not careful. He'd always been that way but eight years of standing behind Bill Clinton as his vice-president had transformed him into the maestro of caution in all his public statements and stances. You never knew what novel adventures the president might lead Gore into or what "prevailing legal authority" might be called on for escape. Yet beyond all those considerations, a deep-rooted ambivalence about joining the family business—politics—continues to feed his naturally hesitant nature. In late July 2000, Gore had watched the bounce in the polls that George W. Bush had received from picking the unexciting but solid Dick Cheney as his choice for second-in-command. Gore now wanted that same spike in the numbers for himself, and as the Democratic convention approached, a careful vetting process by his staff produced a plausible group of candidates. Of those mentioned, House minority leader Dick Gephardt really didn't want the job. Neither did Governor Jeanne Shaheen of New Hampshire. This left a quartet of senators.

John Edwards of North Carolina, a first-termer, was regarded as charismatic but much too inexperienced.

Evan Bayh of Indiana, a veteran with national name recognition, had problems because abortion rights activists did not want to see him nominated. John Kerry of Massachusetts, a likable candidate with broad appeal because of his experience as a Vietnam War hero turned antiwar protester, wasn't perceived as strong enough. That left sturdy Joe Lieberman of Connecticut—the somewhat contrary senator who was known primarily as the first Democrat on the floors of Congress to criticize the president over the Monica Lewinsky affair. He was also an orthodox Jew with an imposing ethical reputation. His record in the Senate, in the face of that reputation, was perhaps a secondary consideration for a presidential candidate looking to distance himself from sexual questions and all sorts of loose behavior. Hollywood didn't like Lieberman much, but, money notwithstanding, how many votes came from that small community? Money, yes, but significant money was already moving toward the Democrats from other directions—the same kind of corporate soft money the Republicans were bringing into their coffers. With or without Hollywood, both parties would probably generate more than $100 million for their respective campaigns.

For eight years President Clinton had put Al Gore in charge of a number of important areas—spheres of influence, they were called in the White House. They included the environment, high-tech issues, tobacco, and disarmament problems for several former Soviet republics. Gore understood his role in shaping these agendas and told the *Washington Post*: "Everything that a Vice-President is able to do depends upon a delegation of authority from the President. Therefore the relationship, and the trust in that relationship, is very important—that's the one key to it." Being in this position of subservience to a president, and particularly to this president, had often made Gore look uncertain, insecure, defensive, until there were times when he appeared almost literally frozen in place.

So his selection of Lieberman had numerous benefits: He got to appear daring, sure-handed, unpredictable, and committed to high ethical standards, while also looking, according to the *Washington Post*, "pleasing to the media and the political elite."

Having spent most of the past decade as the semi-muzzled number-two man in the White House, Gore could certainly appreciate what Lieberman's future might hold if the pair were elected in November. He trusted that the senator would wear the same kind of muzzle Gore had worn while sublimating his own past political independence to support Gore's initiatives and programs. And Gore knew one other thing as well, something that carried with it real historical weight: If he won the 2000 presidency and served two terms, he would provide Lieberman with the perfect springboard from which to run for president himself, the first time a Jewish-American would have ever been in that position. Gore was in fact opening a large door. Winning the White House on one's own, of course, was entirely different from running as vice-president. Richard Nixon and Gerald Ford had found that out. George Bush had done this—once—before being sent home by the American people.

Al Gore's ride to the nomination had known plenty of potholes. His disorganized attempt to run for president in 1988 had shown a lack of planning and forcefulness, especially when one considers that the Democratic nominee that year was the lightly regarded Michael Dukakis. Gore's campaign had also ended $2 million in debt. Four years later, as he watched candidates like Bill Clinton emerge, he had felt regret at not jumping back into the political wars sooner. As he told Larry King on a CNN broadcast: "I may never have a better chance to run than the chance I passed up this time."

In 1992, Gore did not seem anxious to accept the vice-presidential spot from Clinton, but when the nominee's so-called dream choices—Colin Powell and Mario Cuomo—failed to develop, Clinton asked Gore to join him on the ticket. Win or lose, Gore felt that his chances for the top spot in 1996 or 2000 would be enhanced by saying yes. And the "partnership" notion—of shared duties for both the president and the vice-president—which Clinton had been touting, intrigued Gore. Maybe he could be a vice-president who actually did something.

Warren Christopher vetted Gore (as he later would vet Lieberman in 2000) and gave him a positive recommendation. Clinton was pleased because he felt that he needed Gore to win the election and that the senator from Tennessee would be a loyalist in a Clinton White House. The president-elect turned out to be a prophet on both counts.

Many Gore staffers received appointments from Clinton—cabinet posts, significant White House posts, and administrative agency chairmanships. Gore had eyes and ears everywhere in the administration, and the president rarely made a major move without talking to him. But Clinton's stumbles often left Gore involved in damage control rather than policy initiatives. The vice-president was an expert counter-puncher and Clinton continually used him in that role. Whatever his private frustration, Gore played the good-soldier role and said nothing negative—at least for public consumption. It is interesting to remember that during many of the most feverish moments of the Lewinsky matter, Gore was not to be found in Washington, D.C.

Now that Gore was finally on his own in 2000, his challenges were sticky indeed. He needed to attach himself to the eight years of unparalleled growth and prosperity the country had been through under Clinton—by promising four more years of the same. He also needed to activate the "Who wants to switch horses in midstream?" button and push this often. Yet at the same time he wanted to use the Lieberman pick to show the nation that he did not approve of Clinton's behavior in the Monica Lewinsky affair. Choosing the Democrats' straightest shooter was intended to mean that he would bring a high moral tone to the White House and there would be no hanky-panky in his administration. Yet turning his back on President Clinton was not a simple or necessarily smart thing to do. Gore and Clinton were good friends and the nominee greatly desired access to the Clinton donor base. The president from Arkansas was without doubt the most prodigious fund raiser ever to occupy the White House and, clearly, Gore wanted some of those donations to fall his way.

Gore's selection of Lieberman carried with it some ironies, some risks, and some as-yet-unknown results. Long ago the nation seemed to want to put the Clinton-Lewinsky mess behind it, yet by choosing Lieberman as his vice-president, Gore had thrust the scandal back into the spotlight. People were suddenly talking less about him and his political ideas than about how the scandal would play in the upcoming election. While Gore seemed desperately to want to set the sex issue aside for good, his decision has done nothing but cause it to reemerge. It was impossible to say whether Lieberman's high-mindedness could offset the fact that many Americans, including many Democrats who did not live on either coast and were not knowledgeable about Orthodox Judaism ("yellow dog" Democrats, as some of the more rural ones had once been called), doubted whether Lieberman could help them win the election, when the polls suggested that their candidate was trailing badly.

Would the senator truly broaden Gore's appeal and bring in votes that would otherwise have been cast for George W. Bush? Or would he only captivate those who were already behind Gore? This was the great question inside the great experiment of naming Lieberman the Democratic nominee in the first national election of the new millennium.

The answer could be historic.

7

Religion

Senator Lieberman, as quoted on the website Religion Today.com, responded to Al Gore's telephone request to become Gore's running mate in an openly religious way. "We shared a short prayer together," the senator told the Associated Press. His mention of this prayer was among the first signs that Lieberman's religious views would be openly expressed and, as a result, probably much debated by American voters and observers to American politics around the world.

"Vice President Al Gore's selection of Senator Joseph Lieberman is the political equivalent of landing a man on the moon," stated Rabbi Marvin Hier, dean and founder of the Simon Wiesenthal Center, in a press release on August 8, 2000. "America will never be the same. It finally puts to rest the taboos that a person's religious or ethnic background should prevent him from seeking the highest office in the land. John Kennedy put that taboo to rest for Catholics and Joseph Lieberman has done the same for the Jews. This is a great triumph for American democracy."

This comparison between the barrier broken by President John F. Kennedy, the first Catholic to be nominated for executive office, and Senator Lieberman, the first Jewish person to run on the national ticket of a major political party, has been made by many people. Vice President and presidential candidate Al Gore, as part of his August 8, 2000, speech announcing Lieberman as his running mate, invoked Kennedy. Referring to the Democratic Convention, Gore said, "Next week, when our party meets in Los Angeles, we will recall the last time we met there, at the convention where we nominated John F. Kennedy. That year, we voted with our hearts to make history by tearing down an old wall of division. And when we nominate Joe Lieberman for vice-president, we will make history again. We will tear down an old wall of division once again."

Kennedy himself presaged Lieberman's position in his remarks to the Greater Houston Ministerial Association on September 12, 1960, transcribed in Theodore White's book about the road to Kennedy's election, *The Making of the President 1960*, published by Buccaneer Books. The then-presidential candidate said, "While this year it might be a Catholic against whom the finger of suspicion is pointed, in other years it has been, and may someday be again, a Jew—or a Quaker—or a Unitarian—or a Baptist. It was Virginia's harassment of Baptist preachers, for example, that led to Jefferson's statute of religious freedom. Today I may be the victim—but tomorrow it may be you." His statements are very relevant today, as evidenced by the broadcast of parts of the speech on NPR's "Morning Edition" on August 10, 2000.

There is one outstanding difference between the situation Kennedy faced and Lieberman's, beyond the differences between a nomination for president and a nomination for vice-president. In 1957, the Catholic population in the United States was between 20 percent and 26 percent, according to *The Making of the President*. Today, according to the *CIA World Factbook 1999*, 28 percent of Americans are Roman Catholic, so the percentages are very similar. Also according to *CIA World Factbook 1999*, only 2 percent of Americans are Jewish. It stands to reason that the average non-Jewish person would have much less exposure to Judaism than the average non-Catholic to Catholicism.

Rabbi Joseph Ehrenkranz, the influential rabbi of Lieberman's youth who believes Lieberman would make a "superb vice-president, if not the best," agrees with the common perception that most Americans are not very familiar with Judaism. Rabbi Ehrenkranz stated that "those people in big cities with large Jewish populations should know about Judaism from their neighbors, but even then there may be some Jews who don't have complete knowledge of Judaism, though it's not a complicated religion. Judaism is just Biblical, with very strong beliefs in the Word of God."

Ignorance and Anti-Semitism

"If you get away from the two coasts, there's a lot of territory where being Jewish remains a curiosity," according to David Corn, Washington editor of *The Nation*, as quoted in the *Hartford Courant* on August 9, 2000. "It's not that people are anti-Semitic, but Judaism is something foreign to them. It is noteworthy and newsworthy."

Herbert J. Muller, in *The Uses of the Past: Profiles of Former Societies*, published by Oxford University Press, muses on how Christians view Jews, and draws a dark historical conclusion. "Within a century or so [of the point when Christians broke away from Judaism] Christians knew nothing about the living religion of Israel . . . treating it as a poor, wayward relation rather than an elder brother."

Also important to take into account, according to Rabbi Ehrenkranz, is the fact that Judaism is "absolutely not evangelical." Rabbi Ehrenkranz points to the Jewish belief that every human is entitled to salvation, thus the need to convert others in order to save them is nonexistent for Jews. Part of the result of that broad and accepting view is there is little exposure of non-Jews to Judaism by the means that many Americans are exposed to other, more evangelical faiths. Rabbi Ehrenkranz believes that the common misconception that Judaism is "very restrictive" is a symptom of most Americans' general lack of knowledge about the religion, as is the ignorant, dim view of the anti-Semite.

What does this mean for Lieberman? In a press release on August 7, 2000, Abraham H. Foxman, national director of the Anti-Defamation League (ADL), stated: "The choice of Sen. Joe Lieberman as a Vice Presidential candidate is a milestone in America's political maturity." He continued: "While anti-Semites and those on the fringe of society who subscribe to conspiracy theories may have a field day with the choice of Sen. Lieberman, we remain confident that the American people will dismiss the extremists and consider him on his public record."

There may be encouraging news for those in the Gore/Lieberman camp who are concerned about anti-Semitism affecting the vote. According to a Gallup poll quoted by Hanna Rosin in the August 9, 2000, *Washington Post*, 92 percent of Americans polled said they would be "comfortable voting for a Jewish president, compared to 37 percent in the mid-1940's."

However, since the announcement of Lieberman's selection as Gore's running mate, anti-Semitic e-mails and comments have appeared. America Online (AOL) recorded more than 28,000 postings on Lieberman within forty-eight hours of the announcement. According to the Associated Press, AOL deleted an unspecified number of these messages because they violated its policies against hate speech. In addition, the AP reported that CNN suspended about ten users from its chat rooms. Also, the *New York Times* reported on August 8, 2000, that a chat room about the Lieberman selection drew 14,000 postings. At times, half were attacking Lieberman's religion. It is worth noting that no less prominent a commentator than radio's Don Imus, in a broadcast on August 11, 2000, expressed the possibility that no matter what people might say publicly or in opinion polls, at the end of the day significant numbers of them might simply refuse to vote a Jewish person into such high office.

Rabbi Ehrenkranz gave Lieberman some optimistic advice on the subject, in keeping with the optimism of his faith. He told him, "You're not going to win Wyoming or Texas, but there are 48 more states in this country. There are crazy bigots in each of our fifty states, but in each of those states they are a very small minority of very ignorant people. Also in each of those states are many reasonable people who want to bring the best person to the position of vice president."

Lieberman reflected this advice when he addressed the topic on CNN's "Larry King Live" on August 8, 2000, saying that he trusted the tolerance of the American people to ensure that people will judge him as a person with regard to whether he can perform the job of the vice-president, rather than judging him based on his religion.

Judaism

If the best antidote to ignorance is information, it is fortunate that so much information about Judaism is available from myriad sources, including many websites. An overview of Judaism is useful in grasping Lieberman's religion and how it informs his values, views, and, as has been much discussed, his schedule.

As defined by the website Encyclopedia.com, Judaism is a religion of monotheism. The worship of the one true God is central to the religion. Study of the Written Torah, or the Pentateuch, which is comprised of the first five books of the Bible, is fundamental to Jewish life, according to the Jewish Community Online. The site's definition continues, "The Torah is the first of three parts of the Hebrew Bible, the Tanakh, which is, basically, what non-Jews would call the Old Testament." The two terms are not interchangeable, however. "The main differences between the Tanakh and the Old Testament are 1) Jews don't use the term Old Testament, 2) the books in the Tanakh and what non-Jews call the Old Testament are not in the same order and 3) there are some pretty major disagreements about translation." The five books of the Torah are Genesis, Exodus, Leviticus, Numbers, and Deuteronomy.

The Ten Commandments "are accepted by Judaism and Christianity as a summary of the important rules of behavior that God expects of humanity," states religioustolerance.org. They are given in Chapter 20 of the Book of Exodus.

The next two sections of the Jewish Bible are *N'viim*

(Prophets) and *K'Tuvim* (Writings), according to Shamash. org, the Jewish Internet Consortium. These include the books of the Old Testament, but as stated by the Jewish Community Online, the order and interpretation of these books is very different.

Lieberman, and rabbis asked about Lieberman, have referred to the teachings in the Talmud. What is the Talmud? In *Essential Judaism: A Complete Guide to Beliefs, Customs, and Rituals*, published by Pocket Books, author George Robinson explains, "The Bible is the cornerstone. The Talmud is the foundation." He continues, "The Talmud is unlike any other religious book ever compiled. . . . One could spend a lifetime studying it and never master its complexities."

Clearly it is an intricate document. Robinson writes, "Reduced to its simplest form, the Talmud consists of two parts. The first, the *Mishnah*, is an analysis, in Hebrew, of biblical law, of the *mitzvot*, as it emerges from the *praxis* of the rabbis. . . . The second part of the Talmud is *Gemara*, rabbinic commentaries, mostly in Arabic, on *Mishnah* that attempt to elucidate that earlier work." Robinson summarizes by stating, "In short, the key texts . . . constitute an elaborate debate—across generations, across millennia—about the nature of Jewish law, ritual, observance."

Posted on About.com is a famous story from the Talmud that "best summarizes the essence of Judaism. A non-Jew asked Rabbi Hillel to teach him all about the Torah while standing on one foot. Rabbi Hillel said: 'What is hateful to you, don't do unto your neighbor. The rest is commentary. Now, go and study.' "

The Rabbi

The significance of the role of the rabbi in the life of a member of a Jewish congregation is difficult to overestimate. The rabbi is more than a speaker, more than an interpreter, and more than a counselor. As Rabbi Milton Steinberg explains in his book *Basic Judaism*, published by Harcourt Brace, "Rabbis are teachers of the Tradition. They are generally called on to discharge additional functions as pastors, preachers, administrators, and communal leaders. But first and foremost they are teachers. This is the essence of their being."

While rabbis are available for counseling and to communicate learned interpretations of Jewish texts, Rabbi Ehrenkranz states that Lieberman has not come to him for counseling on enormous issues in his political career like the confirmation of Clarence Thomas for the U.S. Supreme Court or his public denouncement of President Clinton for his affair with Monica Lewinsky. In fact, Lieberman has come to Ehrenkranz only after he has made such decisions or given his votes to discuss what he did after the fact.

Prayer

Communication with God is very important. The ritual of prayer includes the recitation of certain key prayers both at home and in the synagogue. "Prayer is one of the main forms of Jewish spiritual and religious identity," states Professor David Blumenthal in an introduction to a class on Rabbinic Judaism, "Prayer and Liturgy" at Emory University.

Diet

OU.org offers an explanation of the rules governing the dietary options for observant Jews—the rules for keeping *kosher*. "The Hebrew word *kosher* means fit or proper as it relates to dietary (kosher) laws. It means that a given product is permitted and acceptable. The sources for the laws of kashruth are of Biblical origin and expounded in Rabbinic legislation, through which the Rabbis interpreted, or added preventative measures to the Biblical regulations. These laws are codified in the Shulchan Aruch (Code of Jewish Law), and are discussed in the ancient, medieval, and contemporary writings of the Rabbis."

Governed by kosher guidelines are many elements of food preparation and consumption. Only certain meats are allowed; for instance, of all mammals only the meat of those that chew their cud and have cloven hooves is suitable for consumption. There are strict rules about the method of slaughtering and salting meats. Also, meat and dairy items must be kept separate, and one must have separate utensils, including flatware, cookware, and dishes, for the handling of each. There are many provisions for the preparation of bread and pastries, which in anything greater than a one-serving size must not contain dairy products.

Keeping kosher is a challenge, but many options are open to Jews, even at public gatherings where special arrangements for the presentation of kosher food have not been made. Rabbi Ehrenkranz sees the common buffet table as a particularly good solution, as no one is required to make special requests, and there is always plenty on such a buffet that would qualify as kosher, especially in a salad section.

Jewish Holidays

Jewish holidays are very important to the religious life of Jews. The **Sabbath**, or *Shabbat*, is extremely significant to Orthodox Jews. As with other Bible-based religions and denominations, the Sabbath in Judaism marks the seventh day, the day that God rested according to the Bible after he completed his Creation. Jews commemorate the Sabbath in various ways, according to their personal interpretations of its meaning. Many Orthodox Jews do so according to Jewish teachings by withdrawing from the "machinery" of the contemporary world into contemplation of the gifts of God.

Significantly, the Sabbath is the only holiday mentioned in the Ten Commandments. The Fourth Commandment, as posted on Bible.ort.org, reads, "Remember the Sabbath to keep it holy. You can work during the six weekdays and do all your tasks. But Saturday is the Sabbath to God your Lord. Do not do anything that constitutes work. [This includes] you, your son, your daughter, your slave, your maid, your animal, and the foreigner in your gates. It was during the six weekdays that God made the heaven, the earth, the sea, and all that is in them, but he rested on Saturday. God therefore blessed the Sabbath day and made it holy."

As given on the Union of Orthodox Jewish Congregations of America's website, OU.org, the "Shabbat testifies to the dignity of labor and the basic equality of all human beings. The Torah commands 'Six days shall you labor';—all of you! No exceptions! Yet, all members of the household, all classes of society, from the king to the servant; even the animals, are to be provided with a 'Day of Rest.' " The Sabbath occurs every seventh day—from sundown Friday to sundown Saturday.

Rosh Hashanah, also called the Jewish New Year, is, according to About.com, "a time to begin introspection. Jews look back at the mistakes of the past year and make resolutions for the new year. The themes of the festival are repentance, preparation for the day of Divine judgment and prayer for a fruitful year. Major customs of

Rosh Hashanah include the sounding of the *shofar* [a ram's horn] during lengthy prayer services, elaborate meals, and no work."

As with many holidays, Jewish holidays occur on different dates each year, depending on where the traditional Jewish calendar places the holidays in the secular calendar. Rosh Hashanah takes place in September. The days between Rosh Hashanah and Yom Kippur are called the Days of Awe.

Yom Kippur, or the Day of Atonement, is, according to Virtual Jerusalem's vjholidays.com, "the day on which Moses descended from Mt. Sinai with the second Tablets of Stone, forty days after the collective sin of the Golden Calf." The sin of idolatry by the Israelites was atoned for on Yom Kippur, which Shamash.org calls "the holiest and most solemn day of the year." Yom Kippur occurs in September or early October, and is preceded by ten days of repentance. On Yom Kippur, Jews fast and attend services.

Hanukah is the "Hebrew word for dedication," according to EverythingJewish.com. It is an eight-day celebration in December, commemorating the Jews' struggle for the freedom to practice their religion, and the victory of the Jews over the Syrians in biblical times, a battle in which the Jews were greatly outnumbered. Many Christians are familiar with Hanukah because of its proximity on the calendar to Christmas.

Passover, or the "Feast of Freedom" as introduced by EverythingJewish.com, celebrates the Exodus of the Jews from Egypt after having been freed from slavery to the Egyptian pharaoh. It commemorates the birth of the Jewish nation. Passover occurs in April, nearly coinciding with the Christian celebration of Easter. The culmination of the celebration of Passover is the *Seder*, a feast that features a communal retelling of the story of the Exodus.

These are not all the Jewish holidays. More than fifteen other holidays are celebrated by Jews, carrying on traditions that go back for millennia.

Orthodox Judaism

Beyond being Jewish, Lieberman was raised and is an Orthodox Jew, which has compelled people to ask many questions, since still fewer Americans are familiar with Jewish Orthodoxy. Shamash.org lists the "core beliefs of Orthodox Judaism," as found in the "Thirteen Principles of Faith" given by Rabbi Moses Maimonides, as:

1. G-d's Existence
2. G-d is a complete and total unity
3. G-d is not physical
4. G-d is eternal and the First Source
5. Prayers should be directed to G-d
6. G-d communicates with man
7. Moses' prophecy is unique
8. The entire Torah is G-d-given
9. The Torah is unchangeable
10. G-d knows man's thoughts and deeds
11. Reward and punishment
12. The Messiah will come
13. The dead will live again

(An admonition in Deuteronomy not to erase or deface the name of God in vain precludes, for many Jews, the actual, entire spelling of the name of God, according to clickonjudaism.com. Therefore, God is often written "G-d" in Jewish papers, as in the preceding section.)

Shamash.org also offers the explanation that "one of

the hallmarks of Orthodox Jews is an openness (and encouragement) to question what it is that G-d requires of us, and then to answer those questions within the system that G-d gave us." In addition, Rabbi Ehrenkranz states that Orthodox Jews believe in the authenticity of the Bible.

The Role of Women in Orthodoxy

This leads into another issue arising from the public's lack of knowledge about Lieberman's particular faith— the role of women in Jewish Orthodoxy. Traditionally, the Jewish woman's role is in the home, not in the synagogue, where women are forbidden by Orthodox Judaism to sit with the men, as explained in a piece in the August 8, 2000, edition of *The New London Day* by Steven Slosberg. Slosberg ruminates on the possibility that Lieberman is "likely to provoke questions about this seemingly secondary and decidedly domestic role for women . . . as a candidate for the nation's second highest office."

Rabbi Ehrenkranz offers a response that stresses the ongoing evolution of the interpretations of the Talmud by Orthodox Jews. He believes that the role of women in society has changed so much and so drastically during the past century, along with attitudes toward the roles of women, that Orthodox Jewish interpretations of the teachings concerning the roles of women will change as well. It is just a matter of time.

He points out that Golda Meir would never have been elected the fourth prime minister of Israel in 1969 had attitudes and interpretations not evolved over time to the point where voting for her, even as an Orthodox Jew, was conceivable.

Hadassah Lieberman herself stands out as an example

of today's Orthodox Jewish woman. She works, and, according an August 9, 2000, story by Carrie Melago in the *New Haven Register*, she "has struggled to find jobs that won't conflict with her husband's role, leaving a post at a public affairs firm, APCO Worldwide in Washington, DC, that did lobbying." The story includes descriptions of how friends see Mrs. Lieberman as a woman of integrity and honesty. The piece relays a report that in 1998 Mrs. Lieberman discouraged her husband from publicly denouncing President Clinton for his affair with Monica Lewinsky, saying that it would be inappropriate for a Jewish senator to do so.

Divorce

What is inappropriate for Jews? It is generally true that the more strict adherents become in observing their faith, the more shame is attached to such common occurrences as divorce. However, in Judaism, according to Rabbi Ehrenkranz, there are no restrictions on divorce, and there is no shame attached.

In the case of Senator Lieberman's divorce from his first wife, Betty Haas, in 1981, there is little fodder for those who might try to find something of which the senator should be ashamed. The two divorced on friendly terms. There was no scandal, and they worked out shared custody terms for their two children, agreeing, according to an August 9, 2000, piece by Susan A. Zavadsky in the *New Haven Register,* to share custody and expenses for children and remain living near one another to prevent the divorce from interfering with the children's schooling. Ms. Haas was quoted in the article as endorsing Lieberman as the vice-presidential candidate, saying "I'm thrilled and excited, and I think he'll make a fine vice-president."

Alcohol

It is well noted that Lieberman's father ran a liquor store. Does this conflict with Jewish teachings, as it might with other conservative doctrines? Rabbi Ehrenkranz emphasizes that alcohol plays a role in many temple services, and states that there is no restriction on the sale or consumption of alcohol by members of the Jewish faith.

Abortion

This is a tricky topic for today's politicians. Judaism offers a unique perspective, differing from other faiths in its allowance for a woman to make such a decision on her own while not endorsing "abortion at will." The faith believes a woman should be able to choose to abort if she feels the pregnancy will "impair her health," and asserts that this is a decision only the individual woman—not disinterested parties, not even the man who impregnated her—can make. Therefore, legislation against abortion is not in keeping with this set of beliefs.

Capital Punishment

Biblically, the belief is in the requirement of an "eye for an eye, a tooth for a tooth." Exodus 21:14 in an English translation of the Torah on Bible.ort.org reads, "If a person plots against his neighbor to kill him intentionally, then you must even take him from My altar to put him to death." However, what amounts to proof that a person has killed and killed in a fashion that allows for the state to take his life in return may be different for the conscience of the Jewish faith and for the U.S. judicial system.

If proper proof is attained, the death penalty could be

an acceptable punishment for certain convicted criminals, according to Rabbi Ehrenkranz.

Equality

The idealism of Jewish teachings equals a firm belief in the equal treatment of all people under the law. As stated in *Basic Judaism*, "Are all men equal before God? Then there must be but one law . . . and justice may not be perverted whether out of deference toward the rich or out of sympathy for the poor."

The Role of Man, and Lieberman

Rabbi Ehrenkranz is warmly, enthusiastically supportive of Lieberman. "The Jewish religion is a religion of optimism. When he completed his Creation, God saw the world as very good. Despite his knowing that there would be wars, bigotry, hatred, greed, God saw the potential in the world. We must see that potential. Also, when God created the world, he gave it to mankind and instructed man to fulfill it—that is man's role. He put us in an imperfect world. It is for man to complete. I see Joe Lieberman as part of the fulfillment of that prophecy.

"Further, God created man in His image—each of us has God within him. The way we treat our fellow humans is how we treat God." He also expresses the importance in Jewish teachings of protecting the environment, a key issue for Lieberman. "God placed man in the Garden and said, 'Make this world a Garden. It's a Paradise if you work and watch over it.' It isn't God who pollutes the world, it's man."

Lieberman's Observances

Senator Joseph Lieberman lives by his faith, as does his family. It is at the core of his being, a fact he discusses

openly. He is observant. He keeps the Sabbath. The day
of rest is very significant for Lieberman and his family.
In his book *In Praise of Public Life*, published by
Simon & Schuster, Lieberman describes the importance
of the Sabbath to him. "It is a day apart, when my family
and I are able to reconnect with one another and with our
spiritual selves, to pray, to talk, to read, to rest or to just
plain enjoy ourselves. It is a 'time beyond time,' as one
rabbi called it. In fact, I don't usually wear a watch on
the Sabbath."

According to an article by Jennifer Walsh in the August 9, 2000, *Boston Globe*, Lieberman refrains from
many activities during the Sabbath. Lieberman does not
work. He doesn't drive, and he doesn't write. In addition,
it has been widely reported that he doesn't watch television or listen to the radio, he doesn't talk on the telephone, and he goes further than simply not driving—he
is also not driven. The Sabbath is his time to consider the
greatness of God's creation and to be thankful for all he
has been given. He spends the Sabbath with his family in
quiet contemplation.

In a piece by Andrea Stone in the August 8, 2000,
USA Today, there is an account of Lieberman's having
consulted with his rabbi about working on the Sabbath.
"Can he work on Saturday, the Jewish Sabbath, when it
is forbidden to drive or spend money, Lieberman wanted
to know. If there's a Saturday vote, is it better to have an
aide drive him, or should he take the subway and let the
aide insert the farecard? 'We decided it was better to take
the Metro because it's running anyway,' says Rabbi
Barry Freundel of Kesher Israel, the Georgetown synagogue that Lieberman and his family attend every Saturday when he's in town."

In fact, Lieberman sat out Connecticut's 1988 Democratic Convention, where he would be nominated as the Democratic candidate for the U.S. Senate, a seat he would go on to win after a long battle against incumbent Lowell Weicker, Jr. According to an August 8, 2000, story posted on ABCNews.com, he didn't attend the convention because it occurred on the Sabbath, and the event was entirely political. The story goes on to state that Lieberman hasn't said whether he would be willing to campaign, which is an entirely political activity, on the major Jewish holidays.

During his August 8 interview on "Larry King Live," he explained: "Politics is politics, which I don't do on the Sabbath, because I think respecting the Sabbath and honoring the Fourth Commandment of the 10 is more important. But when it comes to governmental responsibility, I have always felt—and the Rabbis have encouraged me in this—and Jewish tradition does—that when you have a responsibility to people that can protect or advance their well-being or their lives, then you have got to do it. If the Sabbath is about respecting creation and honoring and protecting human life, then how could you let the specific prohibitions of the Sabbath stop you from doing that? So I voted on the Sabbath. The vote on the Gulf War resolution was on a Saturday. And of course I was there." This is only one of the Saturday votes in the Senate for which Lieberman has been present. Robert McFadden, in an August 8, 2000, piece for the *New York Times*, puts the number of Saturday votes by Lieberman at seventy-five.

This is possible, in spite of his Orthodox observances, because he is acting for the public good, an allowance made by the Talmud. Orthodox Jewish doctors can operate on Saturdays because of this allowance. However, Lieberman does not break with the other restrictions on such Saturdays. There are numerous accounts of his walking to the Capitol, nearly five miles from his home, to be present when needed, then walking back.

When asked about reconciling the demands on him as a public official with his observance of the Sabbath, in an interview with Judith Shulevitz in the "Culturebox" section of *Slate* on March 29, 2000, Lieberman said, "I feel I've reached a conclusion on these questions that I'm comfortable with." He stated that, regarding meeting with "world leaders or members of the Cabinet," he would "try to schedule them some other time, but if something needed to be done, I'd do it."

Lieberman also explained his allowance for work on the Sabbath for "governmental or public responsibility" by saying, "You come to a point where you have to decide whether your rigid observance of the ritual puts you in a position of failing to uphold an ethical value that is also central to your religion." Lieberman's view is reinforced by Rabbi Ehrenkranz, who explains that a Jewish person is bound by Jewish law to work for the betterment of his or her nation.

His fellow senators and members of Congress are familiar with his devoutness, and he is respected for it. He does not thrust his religious views upon others, and is respected for this as well, perhaps even more. While he and his family order their lives around the teachings of the Talmud and the Torah, he neither implies nor expects that his partners in government do so.

Separation of Religion and Policy, Church and State

As a senator, Lieberman has earned a reputation of fairness, of equal emphasis on all issues, not just "Jewish" issues. There is concern that Lieberman as vice-president or (if Gore were incapacitated or worse) as president would be more likely to act on behalf of Israeli interests than would a non-Jewish leader. His voting record does show that he is pro-Israel, but he has also voted in favor of the sale of arms to Saudi Arabia, demonstrating that his motivations where Middle Eastern issues are concerned are clearly more complicated than detractors might like to claim.

Responding to a question posted in the *New York Times* about Lieberman's pro-Israel leanings and how his religion might impact policy in the Middle East, *Time Magazine*'s Tony Karon wrote on the magazine's website on August 10, 2000, that this was a misplaced concern for two reasons. First, "President Clinton's entire National Security team—Albright, Berger, Cohen—are of Jewish origin, as are many of the other key players in his Mideast policy. . . ." Second, he wonders whether any administration could be more pro-Israel than Clinton's. Ultimately, Karon concludes that "Lieberman's qualifications . . . won't be determined by his ethnicity as much as by the depth of his wisdom, both Talmudic and secular."

On the CNN program "TalkBack Live," Senator Charles (Chuck) Schumer, a Democrat from New York, stressed Lieberman's ability to separate the issues of his Jewish religion from the issues before the Senate and how this ability would carry over into the vice-presidency. He said, "I've been close to Joe Lieberman. It hasn't interfered with his duties as senator, and I don't think it will interfere with his duties in any way." On the same program, Rabbi Joseph Potasnik of the Congregation Mt. Sinai in Brooklyn Heights pointed out that while Lieberman's constituency is overwhelmingly non-

Jewish, he has represented the interests of the state as a whole, not just the interests of the state's Jewish population. He stated, "Joe Lieberman represents Connecticut. Some 3 percent of Connecticut is Jewish, 97 percent non-Jews. Some people are atheist, [but] they have no problem with Joe Lieberman because they respect him as a person."

Lieberman commented on whether his religion would ever dictate public policy in an interview on ABC's "Good Morning America" on August 9, 2000. "When I put my hand on that Bible and swear to uphold the Constitution, that is not only a legal obligation I'm accepting, but I'm really swearing to God, and to take the Lord's name in vain has consequences beyond the law. So there's no conflict." Lieberman mentioned his faith numerous times during his speech following Gore's announcement. When asked during the same interview whether a conservative Christian Republican candidate mentioning his faith as many times in such a speech would cause concern and even "alarm" among members of the Democratic Party, Lieberman replied, "I don't think so. . . . But, you know, that's freedom of religion. I'm an individual. I have a right, as every American does, to speak words of faith when the spirit moves me. But that's quite different from doing so as a matter of law."

The religious references in his speech stirred some concern. Americans United for Separation of Church and State issued a press release on August 9, 2000, that stated the group's view on the current debate about "the relationship between faith and politics." The statement continues, "As the campaign proceeds, many voters would be concerned if the senator—or any other candidate—continued to open his appearances with a prayer and a scripture reading."

During an ABCNews.com live chat on August 8, 2000, Connecticut representative John Larson, who has worked with Lieberman in various public offices for more than two decades, expressed succinctly his belief on the subject. Larson said, "Joe Lieberman clearly understands the separation of church and state."

A Worthy Candidate

Lieberman says, in a welcoming audio clip on his official website, that he believes "government should work for the people." He clearly means that it should work for all people, not just those whose demographic groups he falls into, or whose demographic groups his influential voters fall into. The sentiment that he is a fair politician and a good man echoes through the streets of New Haven, Connecticut, where his legions of supporters, won through three decades of dedicated public service, speak freely on his behalf. He is very popular in this mostly non-Jewish state, where the population knows him and knows how he votes, where they've benefited from his advocacy as state senator, attorney general, and U.S. senator—a powerful testament to his religious impartiality.

As a man with a reputation as a morally centered individual amid the swirl of Washington politics, Lieberman might be able to transcend anti-Semitic attitudes and any lack of understanding of his beliefs simply because people see him as a virtuous man. Representative Larson, when asked during that ABCNews.com chat if Lieberman's religious beliefs would resonate with voters in the Bible Belt, said "Lieberman is a man of faith, and I think that will transcend all religious denominations, so I believe that this will be an asset."

George F. Will, in a piece syndicated by "The Washington Post Writers Group" and published in the August 9, 2000, *New London Day*, quotes Wilfred M. McClay, of the University of Tennessee Chattanooga, who writes in *WQ* (the quarterly published by the Woodrow Wilson International Center for Scholars) that there is "a growing sense that religion may be an indispensable force for the upholding of human dignity and moral order in a world dominated by voracious state bureaucracies and sprawling transnational corporations that are neither effectively accountable to national law nor effectively answerable to well-established codes of behavior."

The idea that Lieberman's religion might make him a more viable candidate is repeated by David Broder, a "Washington Post Writers Group" syndicated columnist, in a piece appearing in the August 10, 2000, edition of the *Bucks County* (Pennsylvania) *Courier Times*. Broder writes, "Lieberman's real strength is the moral character he adds to the Democratic ticket."

All things considered, the consensus among politicians is that Lieberman is a worthy candidate. "As a Jew, as a Democrat and as an American, I am elated with the selection of Joe Lieberman as Al Gore's running mate," said Democratic National Committee General Chair Edward G. Rendell in a news release issued on August 8, 2000. "He is as good a public servant as exists in America today and Al Gore deserves congratulations for caring about what's best for America over playing it safe. Joe Lieberman brings intelligence, integrity and courage to our ticket and I know that he will lead this country well."

Similar comments from Senator John Breaux, a Louisiana Democrat, on NBC's "Today" was quoted in an August 7, 2000, piece by G. Robert Hillman in the *Dallas Morning News*. Breaux's perspective echoed that of many other hopeful Democratic politicians. "I don't think people care so much where he goes to church . . . but just that he has the moral values and principles to lead this country."

Perhaps John F. Kennedy was looking forward to a time when a statement like Breaux's could be actual and true when, in the 1960 speech in Houston, he said, "I believe in an America where religious intolerance will someday end . . . where there is no Catholic vote, no anti-Catholic vote, no bloc voting of any kind, and where Catholics, Protestants and Jews . . . will refrain from those attitudes of disdain and division which have so often marred their works in the past, and promote instead the American ideal of brotherhood."

8

The Candidate

The Announcement

Perhaps George W. Bush had been reading the DLC playbook. Just as the tax-and-spend Democrats had transformed themselves into fiscally responsible New Democrats, Bush seemed determined to remake the Republicans, starting from the outside in. While the campaign platform remained largely the same, the new Republican image was to be radically transformed, presented in a media-ready party convention as carefully planned and meticulously choreographed as a Broadway musical. Instead of Pat Buchanan calling out the pitchfork brigade and declaring cultural war on half the country, there was a blues group wailing for the Republicans. Instead of hard-edged attack rhetoric, the speeches were heavy on compassion and light on conservatism. It was the blockbuster remake of former President Bush's "Message: We Care" gaffe. And the message came through loud and clear.

Some observers expressed cynicism: "Not since we first encountered Anna Nicole Smith has the question,

'Are they for real?' more consumed this nation," wrote Dahlia Lithwick in *Slate*.

Of course, the late-night talk show hosts weighed in:

David Letterman: "Every night of the Republican convention, they had a theme, and tonight the theme was, Let's End This Charade and Get Back to Our Restricted Country Club."

Bill Maher: "There was blacks, Hispanics, more blacks, Native Americans, more blacks. You wouldn't have even known it was a Republican convention except for all the rich white guys in the audience checking for their wallets."

Dennis Miller: "Cheney was hired to help Bush find a qualified VP candidate. And he came up with himself. You know, I guess it really is all in who you know."

But in editorials and on the Sunday talk shows, the convention and particularly Bush's speech were praised with words like "masterful," "excellent," "perfection." The public seemed to agree. An NBC poll taken on the Thursday night of the convention gave Bush an eleven-point lead. A tracking poll of likely voters by Voter.com-Battleground gave Bush an eight-point advantage at the start of the week, which soon grew by ten more points. In the tracking poll, Bush led in every region of the country and among most demographic groups.

As the Republicans enjoyed the accolades, Al Gore was wrapping up a week's vacation, going over the short list for running mate. The names most often mentioned were Sen. John Edwards of North Carolina, Sen. John F. Kerry of Massachusetts, Sen. Joseph I. Lieberman of Connecticut, and House Minority Leader Richard A. Gephardt of Missouri. Indiana Sen. Evan Bayh and New Hampshire Gov. Jeanne Shaheen were also floated as long-shot candidates. Gore gave no hint of the historic announcement he was about to make.

The Candidate

The modern political campaign exists almost entirely on paper, over the airwaves, in electronic bundles streaming through the Internet. It's a media event. No nineteenth-century whistle-stop tours; "retail campaigning"—knocking on doors, like Clinton did for Lieberman in 1970—has died out, even in local races. By taking a look at the first week of media coverage of an event or announcement, one can see a lot about how the next few weeks of the campaign are going to unfold—what will be emphasized by each side, what will be spun and how.

The most common reaction to Lieberman's selection was the discussion of his proven ethics and integrity, and Gore's need of them.

From a *Washington Post* article of August 8, 2000, entitled "Integrity on the Ticket":

"Since the start of his campaign, Vice President Al Gore has sought to identify with President Clinton's policies while distancing himself from his flawed character. In selecting Sen. Joseph Lieberman as his running mate, Mr. Gore managed to advance both objectives. Mr. Lieberman chairs the Democratic Leadership Council, the centrist group that helped develop many Clinton-Gore policies. But he also stands out as the first Democratic senator to have criticized Mr. Clinton during the Lewinsky scandal. This special combination—Clintonism without Clinton—makes Mr. Lieberman an appealing choice. Mr. Lieberman has spent a career in politics, in his native Connecticut and then for 12 years in the Senate. Yet he has maintained a reputation for integrity that is sadly rare in the profession."

From a *Los Angeles Times* story on August 8, 2000, called "Gore's Counterweight":

"He is a man of unquestioned honesty and integrity, judging by the comments of his Senate colleagues, Republicans as well as Democrats.

"The Connecticut senator demonstrated his independent spirit on Sept. 3, 1998, when he took the floor of the upper chamber to condemn the 'disgraceful behavior' of President Clinton in the Monica Lewinsky affair. . . . Lieberman also was outspokenly critical of White House fund-raising abuses during the 1996 reelection campaign.

"Political analysts quickly interpreted the selection as an effort by Gore to declare his independence from Clinton and the president's ethical problems."

From a *St. Louis Post–Dispatch* piece on August 8, 2000, called "Neutralizing the Lewinsky Factor":

"Forget the bridge to the 21st century, President Bill Clinton's attempt at a forward-looking metaphor for his 1996 re-election campaign. The past is the battleground for this year's presidential race.

"With the selection of Dick Cheney as his running mate, George W. Bush evoked the prospect of a restoration, the triumphal return of the Gulf Warriors and a time before the presidency was soiled by a sex scandal. . . .

"Al Gore parries the GOP's thrust with his selection of Sen. Joseph Lieberman of Connecticut. . . . His voting record is moderately liberal. . . . He doesn't seem to have any whoppers in his background—like Mr. Cheney's votes against banning cop-killer bullets or freeing Nelson Mandela. . . .

"Clearly, Mr. Gore hopes that Mr. Lieberman will provide a kind of moral vaccination against Republican attacks. At the same time Mr. Gore is distancing himself from Mr. Clinton's moral lapses, he can associate himself—if he is adroit enough—with Mr. Clinton's considerable successes: eight years of prosperity and peace."

From a *Buffalo News* story on August 9, 2000, headlined "The Lieberman Factor":

"In tapping Connecticut Sen. Joseph Lieberman, Vice President Gore accomplished two goals with one phone call: He helped neutralize the morality issue and simultaneously injected some excitement into his campaign by making a bold and unprecedented pick."

From a *New York Times* piece on August 8, 2000, called "The Lieberman Candidacy":

"Vice President Al Gore's decision to choose Senator Joseph Lieberman of Connecticut as his running mate is certainly the most dramatic move he has made in his presidential campaign, and may turn out to be one of the smartest. It is not just that Mr. Lieberman has been an effective senator. Of far greater significance is that he was the first Democratic senator to denounce President Clinton for 'disgraceful' and 'immoral' conduct in the Lewinsky scandal and for his failure to speak truthfully to the American people about his behavior. . . .

"Mr. Gore's decision was bold in one other respect. Mr. Lieberman will be the first Jew to run on the national ticket of a major party. Recent polls have suggested that religion will not be an important factor when Americans make up their minds in this election. Nevertheless, Mr. Gore is in effect inviting the voters to tear down any remaining barriers against Jewish candidates, much as they did for John F. Kennedy's Catholicism a generation ago."

From the *Post-Standard* of Syracuse, New York, in an August 9, 2000, article entitled, "Clear-Cut Choices:

Joseph Isador Lieberman. *(Illustration by Bill Schmidt)*

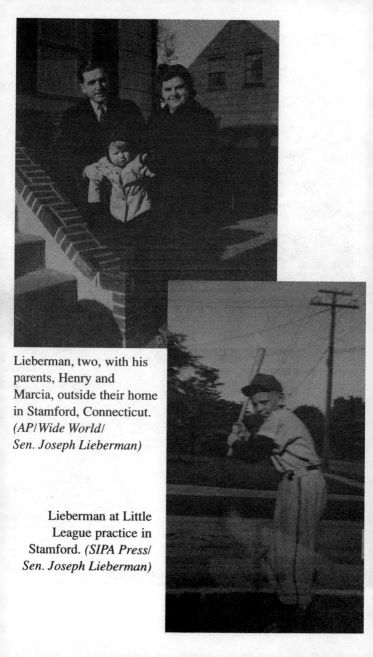

Lieberman, two, with his parents, Henry and Marcia, outside their home in Stamford, Connecticut. *(AP/Wide World/ Sen. Joseph Lieberman)*

Lieberman at Little League practice in Stamford. *(SIPA Press/ Sen. Joseph Lieberman)*

Lieberman as a summer intern for Senator Abraham A. Ribicoff in Washington, D.C. *(AP/Wide World/Sen. Joseph Lieberman)*

Joseph I. Lieberman and his wife, Hadassah.
(SIPA Press/Sen. Joseph Lieberman)

Final rally for his U.S. senate campaign. Hadassah, left,
holding seven-month-old Hana, Lieberman and his mother,
Marcia. *(SIPA Press/Stamford Advocate)*

Just after Lieberman was sworn in as U.S. senator, then
President-Elect George W. Bush met Hana Lieberman, his
nine-month-old daughter. (*AP/Wide World/J. Scott Applewhite*)

Hadassah, Joe, Marcia and Hana in the early 1990s.
(*SIPA Press/Sen. Joseph Lieberman*)

Lieberman and Hana meet Cookie Monster. *(SIPA Press/Sen. Joseph Lieberman)*

Lieberman and his grandaughter, Tennessee Lieberman, two, leaving Sabbath services on August 5, 2000. *(AP/Wide World/ Bob Child)*

Joe and Hadassah jogging near their New Haven, Connecticut home on August 6, 2000. *(AP/Wide World/Bob Child)*

Lieberman's victory
party to celebrate his
election to the
Connecticut State
Senate in 1972.
(CNP/Archive Photos)

Lieberman during a
session of the
Connecticut State
Senate in 1975.
(AP/Wide World)

Lieberman as a State Attorney General delivering a statement about the closing of a local landfill for environmental reasons on April 12, 1984.
(*AP/Wide World/Bob Child*)

Joe Lieberman with President Ronald Reagan. *(Trippett/SIPA Press/Sen. Joseph Lieberman)*

President Bush swears in Lieberman to the U.S. Senate. *(Trippett/SIPA Press/Sen. Joseph Lieberman)*

Lieberman with King Hussein of Jordan.
(Trippett/SIPA Press/Sen. Joseph Lieberman)

Israeli Prime Minister Yitzhak Rabin with Lieberman.
(SIPA Press/Sen. Joseph Lieberman)

Senator Lieberman visits the troops at the front during the Gulf War. *(SIPA Press/Sen. Joseph Lieberman)*

Senator Lieberman applauds his longtime friend President Bill Clinton at the Democratic Leader Council meeting on November 13, 1995. *(AP/Wide World/Wilfredo Lee)*

Lieberman leaving the Old Senate Chambers during the
impeachment trial of President Clinton on August 1, 1999.
(SIPA Press)

A happy and humble Lieberman addresses the press on
August 6, 2000, the day he received the call to become the
first Jewish candidate to run for Vice President.
(AP/Wide World/Steve Miller)

A jubliant Lieberman walks out of his New Haven home on the day after Vice President Al Gore asked him to be his running mate. *(AP/Wide World/Bob Child)*

Lieberman addresses the crowd in downtown Nashville,
Tennessee on August 8, 2000.
(AP/Wide World/Mark Humphrey)

Tipper, Al, Joe and Hadassah begin their long journey to
the White House with confidence. *(AP/Wide World/Mark
Humphrey)*

National Tickets May Look Alike, but Offer Voters Sharp Contrasts in Substance":

"Lieberman was a fascinating choice for a number of reasons. Much has been made of the fact that the Democratic senator from Connecticut is the first Jew to occupy a spot on a national ticket. The fact that this is remarkable is sad commentary on the state of our culture. Anti-Semitism, racism and other forms of prejudice still influence events in American public life.

"In that respect, Gore's decision may be regarded as bold by his supporters and desperate by his critics. To be sure, Lieberman's religion will sway some voters against the Democrats. Anyone who thinks anti-Semitism is but a faint echo of a less enlightened time is naive."

And sure enough—

From a *St. Louis Post—Dispatch* story of August 12, 2000, called "Anti-Semitism's Deep Roots":

"Anti-Semitism? All the speculation about the impact of Sen. Lieberman's religion on voters or on his ability to fulfill the demands of the campaign, the office, and the Torah seemed like idle chatter, strained efforts to dig up some news during the dog days of August.

"But then Lee Alcorn, the president of the Dallas chapter of the NAACP, popped up with this quote on a Texas radio program: 'If we get a Jew person then what I am wondering is, I mean, what is this movement for? . . . We need to be very suspicious of any kind of partnerships between the Jews at that kind of level because we know that their interest primarily has to do with money and these kinds of things.'

"Kweisi Mfume, the NAACP's national president, was quick to denounce Mr. Alcorn's remarks, calling them 'repulsive' and 'anti-American.' But the episode did recall the sometimes troubled relationship between blacks and Jews and the anti-Semitism that sometimes flows through Louis Farrakhan's speeches and interviews. Mr. Alcorn's bigoted comment wasn't an isolated incident.

"After Mr. Gore announced his selection of Mr. Lieberman, anti-Semitic messages began appearing all over in Internet chat rooms. As they customarily do, AOL and CNN responded promptly to the hate speech, suspending the writers from their chat rooms . . . ,

"Without doubt, Mr. Lieberman's candidacy is a rebuke to anti-Semitism and a tribute to the ideal of inclusiveness. But the real challenge of Mr. Lieberman's and Mr. Gore's race may be to take the debate about religion and public life to a different level, one that fully respects the diversity of religious beliefs in this country."

If some commentators felt that Lieberman's nomination signaled an alliance with Israel, others felt precisely the opposite.

From a story in the *Wall Street Journal* on August 9, 2000, entitled, "Lieberman: What's Not to Like? Al Gore's running mate has set himself apart from his party. If only he were more of a fighter."

"I esteem him enormously for his fidelity to Jewish law. And I am not immune from a rush of excitement at the emergence for the first time in 200 years of a Jew on a national ticket—particularly a man who has found his way there not by assimilation but after sticking prominently to his religion. He is a great role model for a generation of young Jewish family builders bucking the demographic trend of a shrinking Jewish community.

"But the fact is that being Jewish doesn't automatically incline one to vote in the way that I have come to root for, to say the least. . . .

"Yet with respect to the issues on which he has been willing to stand apart, he has rarely emerged as a fighter."

Others question the media image of the new candidate:

From a story in the *Houston Chronicle* on August 10, 2000, entitled, "Lieberman moderate? Not the real Joe":

" 'A funny thing happened to me on the way to the state AFL-CIO convention today,' " an elated Sen. Joseph Lieberman told the Connecticut labor gathering in Hartford Monday morning. He meant his selection as Democratic vice-presidential nominee, but what was really 'funny' was revealed a few moments later.

"Embedded in a stock political speech, Lieberman's 180-degree turn on Social Security was hardly noticed. He flipped from New Democrat privatization to Al Gore's stand-pat posture. How could he have changed his mind so quickly? He didn't. Two months ago when Vice President Gore began considering Lieberman as his running mate, Gore aides asked the senator to write out his revised views. He did.

"That fits the real Joe Lieberman. He is one of the best-liked personalities in American politics. But while talking the moderate talk, he walks the liberal walk. The news media description this week of a centrist, moderate or even conservative misrepresented a party regular who more often than not is a conventional liberal."

From an article in *Salon* on August 8, 2000, called "The Two Faces of Joseph Lieberman":

"The reasons for Gore's choice are far deeper, and

rooted in Lieberman's particular success in Connecticut. The story really begins back with Kennedy's taboo-smashing campaign in 1960 . . . in part the work of a Connecticut politician named John Bailey, the Democratic national chairman and Kennedy's close ally. Bailey was a master of political currency, brokering years of patronage and peace between urban ethnic ward bosses and Southern Democrats.

"John Bailey was the young Joe Lieberman's political rabbi. Lieberman, who grew up in a working-class enclave of Stamford, Conn., wrote two books about Bailey and studied carefully the circles of patronage and influence that bound the old Democratic Party together. . . .

"It was Joe Lieberman's unique political insight that the new suburbs required new political currency—a substitute for the patronage system which in the past assured Democratic voters' loyalty. . . .

"Lieberman's blend of suburban environmentalism and social conservatism . . . represent a carefully calculated political persona, which is at the core of Al Gore's own New Democrat faith."

These are issues that will be raised, in various forms and forums, over the next three months, until we discover if Joseph Lieberman becomes a new "first"—the first Jewish vice-president in American history. Throughout his political and personal lives, he's managed to weld together all of his contradictions into the form and substance of a highly successful and well-liked man. Those contradictions have been the driving force of his career and have kept him both interesting and growing as a politician. Whether his personality will stir people who have not made up their minds to vote for Al Gore in November is unknown. No matter if the Democratic ticket wins or loses in the fall, Lieberman's selection as a vice-presidential candidate has widened the experience of the American political scene and broadened our discussion and sense of possibility. This is the real triumph in Gore's choice—at least for now.

Ignorance is the great enemy of hope and the great ally of bigotry and hatred. Each time we learn more about others, we expand our own humanity and sense of connection to the world at large. We stop being quite so afraid. Joe Lieberman has pushed this process along if only by being true to himself and his heritage. That alone is a personal and political victory.

APPENDIX I

The Lieberman Chronicles

1942   Born in Stamford, Connecticut, on February 24 to Henry and Marcia Lieberman.

1950   Moves from grandmother's house near the railroad tracks to Strawberry Hill Court with his parents and two sisters. His mother will live in this house for the next fifty years.

1960   Valedictorian, Stamford High School. Voted "Most Popular." Elected Prom King and Senior Class President.

1960   Enters Yale College.

1962   Named Chairman, *Yale Daily News.* Meets and becomes friendly with John M. Bailey, legendary Connecticut political boss.

1963   Interns with Senator Abraham Ribicoff in Washington. Present when Martin Luther King delivers his "I Have a Dream" speech. Travels to Mississippi to pre-register black voters in preparation for upcoming "Freedom Summer."

1964   Graduates from Yale. Does senior thesis on John Bailey, which wins the Frank M. Patterson Political Science prize. Bailey takes him to the Democratic National Convention in Atlantic City. Enters Yale Law School in the fall.

1965 Marries Elizabeth Haas.

1966 Bailey thesis published as *The Power Broker*.

1967 Son Matt born. Graduates from Yale Law School and becomes an associate with Wiggin & Dana in New Haven. Enters Board of Alderman race but is forced to withdraw because he does not meet city residency requirement.

1969 Daughter Rebecca born. Runs statewide campaign for Robert Kennedy.

1970 Elected to Connecticut State Senate scoring upset win over incumbent majority leader. Houghton-Mifflin publishes *The Scorpion and the Tarantula,* a look at nuclear proliferation efforts.

1972 Starts own law firm, Baldwin & Lieberman. James Segalof joins as a partner the following year. Thayer leaves in 1978. Segalof and Lieberman continue as partners until Lieberman is elected attorney general.

1974 Elected Senate Majority Leader.

1976 Announces interest in running for Lieutenant Governor; loses floor fight for nomination at state convention.

1980 Gives up state senate seat to run for Congress. Enters campaign with large lead and manages to lose. Crushed by unexpected defeat. Wonders if his political career is over.

1981 Publishes *The Legacy,* a history of Connecticut politics from 1930 to 1980. Divorces Betty Haas.

1982 Elected first full-time attorney general. Reorganizes office as consumer defender.

1983 Marries Hadassah Freilich.

1984 Overwhelmingly re-elected attorney general.

1986 Publishes *Child Support in America,* a guide to increasing collection from delinquent fathers.

1988 Runs for U.S. Senate and upsets three-term incumbent Lowell P. Weicker, Jr. His margin of victory is less than 10,000 votes. Daughter Hana born.

1994 Elected to second term. Defeats challenger by nearly 400,000 votes.

1995 Named chairman of the Democratic Leadership Council.

1998 On September 3, excoriates President Clinton in a withering speech from the Senate floor.

1999 Becomes ranking member of the Government Operations Committee

2000 Publishes *In Praise of Public Life*.

2000 Selected by Al Gore as vice-presidential running mate.

APPENDIX II

What People Have Said

Democratic Politicians

Senator Evan Bayh
Democrat–Indiana
official statement—August 7, 2000

"Al Gore has shown tremendous leadership in this historic selection. Senator Joe Lieberman is a wonderful choice. He embodies everything you could want in a Vice Presidential selection: intelligence, integrity, and moral courage. He is clearly qualified to be president.

I have always considered Joe Lieberman a personal role model, and admire his commitment to putting people before partisanship. He is successful because of his willingness to build bipartisan consensus. I personally witnessed the conviction of his principles as we worked together this year on our education reform proposal, and on building the centrist Democratic movement in the Senate.

I admire Joe Lieberman personally and professionally. He is more than a colleague, he is a friend."

Senator John Breaux
Democrat–Louisiana
official statement—August 7, 2000

"Joe Lieberman reflects Americans' desire for moderate, independent-thinking politicians who demonstrate political courage, honesty and integrity. He is a great choice and I commend Vice President Al Gore for his courage in choosing Joe to serve on the Democratic ticket."

Senator Daniel Inouye
Democrat–Hawaii
official statement—August 7, 2000

"Senator Lieberman is an excellent selection. I have enjoyed working with him in the Senate, and I look forward to working with him as the next Vice President of the United States."

Senator Carl Levin
Democrat–Michigan
official statement—August 7, 2000

"Joe Lieberman is a great choice and will make a great Vice President. Senator Lieberman is well respected by members of both parties because he is an independent thinker and someone who builds bridges across the partisan divide in Washington. His selection makes it more likely the campaign will focus on issues because any attempt to link the Democratic ticket to the President's personal failings just won't fly."

Senator John Kerry
Democrat–Massachusetts
as quoted on AlGore2000.com

"[Lieberman is] a proven leader with experience and unquestionable rectitude who shares Al Gore's vision for the country."

Al From
President of the Democratic Leadership Council (DLC)
as quoted on AlGore2000.com

"The choice of a running mate is the first real test of a presidential nominee. By selecting Senator Lieberman, Vice-President Gore has made a clear distinction to look toward the future, rather than the past. As Chairman of the Democratic Leadership Council, Senator Lieberman has helped expand the New Democrat movement across the United States. . . . His presence on the Democratic ticket will undoubtedly strengthen its appeal to supporters of Sen. John McCain and other critical swing voters in the fall election."

Democratic Governor of New Hampshire
Jeanne Shaheen
as quoted on AlGore2000.com

"I think Senator Lieberman is an excellent choice. . . . He's a man of strong character and principle, and he really understands the economy we're in."

Former Senator Sam Nunn
Democrat–Georgia
as quoted on AlGore2000.com

"Joe Lieberman is a leader with strong moral character, integrity and ability. He has made substantial contributions to the United States Senate and to his home state of Connecticut. Joe is a respected leader on defense and foreign policy issues and serves with great distinction and effectiveness as a member of the Senate Armed Services Committee. Over the years, Joe, Bill Bennett and I have shared concerns about the impact that popular culture is having on our nation's young people. I have admired and supported their efforts to improve entertainment content and programming."

Senator Frank Lautenberg
Democrat–New Jersey
as quoted on AlGore2000.com

"Well, I am excited about it. Why? Because Joe Lieberman is someone that everyone respects and for one reason: He is solid in terms of his values. They know he is trustworthy. He has the best opportunity among us to talk on a friendly basis with the Republicans on the other side of the aisle."

Democratic Governor of Delaware Tom Carper
as quoted on AlGore2000.com

"[Lieberman is a] perfect match for America [who] will certainly help our chances of winning the White House this November. . . . Joe Lieberman is a man of unquestionable character, integrity, and intellect. Senator Lieberman is a leader we can trust who has the experience to step in and serve as President if needed."

President Bill Clinton
August 8, 2000
Newsday

"I think he's an extraordinary guy. He's been a friend of mine for 30 years."

State Senator and Majority Leader George Jepsen
Democrat–Stamford, Connecticut
August 8, 2000
The New London Day

"He is the American dream."

Hillary Clinton
First Lady and Democratic Candidate for Senate from
New York
as posted on hillary2000.org

"Joe is a man of incredible ability . . . of ideas and vision. The more the country knows about him the more enthusiastic they're going to be about this choice."

Senator Carl Levin
Democrat–Michigan
August 9, 2000
The Los Angeles Times

"Joe and I have talked about this. He makes people comfortable that he's an American who is Jewish and Orthodox. There is no awkwardness about Joe. He is comfortable with who he is and makes everyone else comfortable."

Edward L. Marcus
Connecticut State Democratic Party Chairman
August 10, 2000
The Litchfield Times

"I think Joe is a person of outstanding integrity, he's intelligent, he's articulate. But I think most importantly, he's a different kind of public figure. He's not flamboyant. He doesn't pound tables or yell or scream. But Joe talks from the heart, and you know that when he says something he really believes it."

Senator Christopher J. Dodd
Democrat–Connecticut
August 10, 2000
The Litchfield Times

"A superb choice [for vice presidential candidate]."

Democratic Consultant Tom O'Donnell
August 12, 2000
The New York Post

"They're talking about Lieberman on sports radio and when that happens, you know you're talking about an event that goes beyond politics."

Republican Politicians

Senator Bob Bennett
Republican–Utah
official statement—August 8, 2000

"Joe Lieberman is a good man, a good senator and a good friend. While I obviously hope and expect George W. Bush to win the presidency, should things go the other way, the country would be better served with Lieberman at the top of the ticket rather than Gore. At least Lieberman had the courage to speak up about Clinton's behavior while Al Gore was defending it. Clearly, Bush's pick of a solid, strong running mate like Dick Cheney forced the Gore camp to cautiously review its own choice for vice president."

Senator Mike Enzi
Republican–Wyoming
official statement—August 8, 2000

"I do respect and like my colleague Senator Lieberman as a person and a capable legislator and I was a guest speaker at a dinner honoring Senator Lieberman soon after I took office.

Ultimately the country will decide this race based on the issues and the philosophy of the candidates, not personalities. Governor Bush believes in more personal freedoms and allowing elected representatives in states, counties, local school boards and towns to decide how to better the lives of people in their own communities without the interference of the massive federal bureaucracy. Al Gore and this administration have run roughshod over individual and states' rights, especially in the

West, they have expanded the role of the federal government and they refuse to allow taxpayers to decide how to spend more of their own money. Even though Sen. Lieberman's record indicates he may have supported a few of Governor Bush's positions, he will be in Vice President Gore's administration and that is what people will have to consider."

Rudolph Giuliani
Republican Mayor of New York
as quoted on AlGore2000.com

"I think he's a very, very good man, a distinguished public servant. I think he's an excellent choice."

Late Senator John Chafee
Republican–Rhode Island
as quoted on AlGore2000.com

"The late Senator Chafee praised Lieberman for being willing to take tough votes to put across a bipartisan centrist stance. 'He's a class act,' Chafee said."

George W. Bush
Republican Governor of Texas and Presidential Candidate
August 10, 2000
The New Haven Register

"I appreciate the strong position on ethics that he's taken. I know he's a man of integrity."

Senator Sam Brownback
Republican–Kansas
August 10, 2000
The Houston Chronicle

"I have often been asked how it is that Joe Lieberman and I are frequent allies in the Senate. . . . On many issues, including supporting missile defense and tort reform, Lieberman has followed his conscience across party lines, making his record on these issues more conservative than Al Gore's. It remains to be seen how the two men's differences will play out as the presidential campaign takes off in earnest."

Non-Politicians

James J. Zogby
President of Arab-American Institute
December 13, 1992
The Washington Post
[referring to Lieberman's putting him in touch with the Clinton campaign]

"Only in America would an Arab American spokesman call a Jewish American senator—to let us help a Southern Baptist get elected President."

Robert A. Hamilton, Journalist
January 28, 1996
The New York Times

"Joseph I. Lieberman was elected to his current office in 1988, and since then has earned a reputation as a moderate Democrat in most areas—excepting entertainment."

Melinda Henneberger, Journalist
June 29, 1997
The New York Times

"Senator Joseph I. Lieberman of Connecticut was the Democrat who was toughest on his fellow party members during hearings of the Senate committee investigating possible campaign finance abuses. . . . Mr. Lieberman has set himself apart at the hearings as easily the least partisan member of a panel given to lawyerly exchanges that translate into: 'You started it.' and 'Did not.' "

Brian Lowry, Journalist
December 15, 1998
The Los Angeles Times

". . . one of the most impassioned cultural warriors."

Deborah Orin, Journalist
March 19, 1999
The New York Post

"Lieberman—like Sens. Daniel Patrick Moynihan (D-N.Y.) and Bob Kerrey (D-Neb.)—is seen as one of the Democratic leaders of conscience and so his views could carry great weight."

Scott Reed
Campaign Manager for Bob Dole's 1996 presidential
campaign
as quoted on AlGore2000.com

"I think it's a bold move."

Rabbi David Rosen
Director of the Israel office of the Anti-Defamation League
(ADL)
as quoted on AlGore2000.com

"It is a mark of maturity for American society that there are no barriers to an individual, regardless of race, color or creed. I think it's a great tribute to the success of the Jewish community in the United States, and I think it's a great tribute to the United States itself."

Jeff Greenfield, CNN
as quoted on AlGore2000.com

"I think of the choices that he had, it is probably . . . the boldest."

William Schneider
Senior Political Analyst for CNN
as quoted on AlGore2000.com

"This is a choice that does reach across party lines, and I think independents will find Joe Lieberman a very appealing candidate."

Jack Rosen
President of American Jewish Congress
as quoted on AlGore2000.com

"It's a historic moment that we can all celebrate. If Senate Lieberman is the choice it will be an indication of how far Americans have come with regard to ethnicity."

Dr. Robert Cox
President of the Sierra Club
as quoted on AlGore2000.com

"The addition of Senator Lieberman makes a strong environmental ticket even stronger—the most pro-environmental ticket in history. Senator Lieberman has consistently voted to protect the environment."

Deb Callahan
President of the League of Conservation Voters (LCV)
as quoted on AlGore2000.com

"With their proven leadership, commitment and record on environmental issues, a Gore/Lieberman ticket promises to make a world of difference for the environment."

Ben Wattenberg, Columnist
on National Public Radio, June 23, 1992
as quoted on AlGore2000.com

"Strong on defense and tough on crime . . . a strong environmentalist and consumerist . . . Lieberman is quality goods."

David Broder, Columnist
January 20, 1995
The Tampa Tribune *Op-Ed*

"Sen. Joe Lieberman is an embodiment and an apostle of a Democratic philosophy that incorporates market-oriented thinking of the Reagan revolution and a muscular defense and foreign policy."

Ellen Sung, Journalist
August 7, 2000
www.policy.com

"Respected as one of the most articulate and principled members of the Senate, Lieberman reached his greatest national prominence in 1998, when he stepped onto the Senate floor and became the first Senate Democrat to publicly castigate President Clinton over his affair with former White House intern Monica Lewinsky."

Rabbi David Avigdor
(Lieberman's neighbor)
August 7, 2000
as quoted by the AP and posted on CNN.com

"He's a wonderful person in his religion, but that's not what Joe Lieberman is all about. He's about families and values and morals."

Abraham Foxman
National Director of the Anti-Defamation League (ADL)
August 8, 2000
as quoted on ctnow.com

"He's the political equivalent of Jackie Robinson for the Jewish community."

Bruce Shapiro, Columnist
August 8, 2000
Salon.com

"[One] Joe Lieberman remains an environmental crusader and consumer rights advocate. Then there is the other Joe Lieberman: The social conservative who won his Senate seat in 1988 with support from William Buckley and other conservative Republicans, running to the right of the civil libertarian and then-Republican Sen. Lowell Weicker. . . . Al Gore wants both Joe Liebermans on his ticket."

Rob Morse, Columnist
August 8, 2000
The San Francisco Examiner

"By picking Lieberman, Gore has hit the Republicans with a big barrel of Shut Up. Shut up about diversity and big tents. Shut up about the need for morality and religion in government. Shut up about Bill Clinton."

Jude Wanniski, Columnist
August 8, 2000
polyconomics.com

"Yes, Lieberman is the kind of fellow who has no enemies, but that's because in the bruising world of party politics, he has never drawn blood. When anyone I know *thinks* of Joe, they think of how he *saved* Bill Clinton from expulsion from office."

William Douglas, Journalist
August 8, 2000
Newsday

"Lieberman has also shown a more conservative edge than Gore. Lieberman has backed capital-gains-tax cuts; he has supported the experimental use of federally funded vouchers to allow parents to send their children to private or religious schools, an idea rejected by Gore."

Anna Schmid
former classmate of Lieberman's
August 8, 2000
The Stamford Advocate

"He carried himself like a president even at Burdick [Junior High]. To think that somebody you went to school with could go that far is great. I'm going to be so proud to vote for him again."

William J. Bennett
Former Secretary of Education and Current Co-Director,
Empower America
August 8, 2000
The New York Times

"He's arguably the best Democrat in the Senate."

Dennis Byrne, Columnist
August 9, 2000
The Chicago Sun-Times

"He's the guy Republican social conservatives repeatedly recruited when they needed a Democrat to add a bipartisan flavor to their latest campaign for public virtues. He's someone respected by many, including myself, even though we disagree with him on some issues."

James Ridgeway, Columnist
August 9–15, 2000
The Village Voice

"Lieberman, known for his Bill Bennett–like moral rectitude (e.g., his public chastisement of Clinton at the height of Monicagate), may assuage some swing Clinton haters, but it's hard to see how he will help shore up the party's minority and working-class base."

John Kass, Journalist
August 9, 2000
The Chicago Tribune

"Lieberman is a political liberal who gets high ratings from liberal policy groups like Americans for Democratic Action. But he's also embraced a few conservative causes too. He's damned Hollywood for brutalizing children and supports radical concepts like education vouchers. And parental notification on abortions.

"Too bad he didn't run for president himself."

Morton Kondracke, Columnist
August 10, 2000
rollcall.com

"Lieberman is such an outstanding figure—even Republicans rushed to praise him—that it's impossible to imagine that a Gore-Lieberman administration would be no different from Clinton-Gore."

Robert Novak, Columnist
August 10, 2000
The Chicago Sun-Times

"He is one of the best-liked personalities in American politics. But while talking the moderate talk, he walks the liberal walk. The news media description this week of a centrist, moderate or even conservative misrepresented a party regular who more often than not is a conventional liberal."

William Safire, Columnist
August 10, 2000
The New York Times

"Lieberman will soon reduce the cognitive dissonance in Jewish Republicans by acting as a normal campaigner, denouncing Bush's team as he did this week as 'the Old Guard that created the problems.' Perhaps 'the conscience of the Senate' will assuage concerns about Gore's unconscionable Asian fund-raising."

Paul Alexander, Journalist
August 10, 2000
from Bloomberg News, as posted on AOL.com

"Lieberman . . . has opposed legislation that has been supported by gay political groups; he voted for the Defense of

Marriage Act of 1996, which opposed same-sex marriages, and sided with Senator Jesse Helms of North Carolina to cut funding to school programs that depict homosexuality in a positive light."

David Broder, Columnist
August 10, 2000
Bucks County Courier-Times

"Lieberman has made himself the most popular politician in either party in his highly competitive, two-party state by dint of character and achievement."

Jonathan Tobin, Columnist
August 11, 2000
The Jewish World Review

"Indeed, Lieberman's reputation as a man of integrity and a moral authority stems in large measure from his willingness to stand out because of public religious observance. His colleagues look up to him because he is an observant Jew, not in spite of it."

Daniel T. Zanoza, Journalist
August 11, 2000
The Chicago Tribune

"The scandal-filled administration, of which Gore is an integral part, has left a very bad taste in the mouths of the electorate. You might call it an integrity gap, which the selection of Lieberman was meant to address . . . he is a man of great integrity and moral conviction."

Noah benShea, philosopher and author
August 11, 2000
The Los Angeles Times

"The difference between a politician and a leader is that a politician thinks about the next election and a leader thinks about the next generation. In Lieberman, you have a leader. The Talmud reminds us that it is a great mitzvah to plant a tree you will never eat the fruit of—not acting for your own aggrandizement. Lieberman is well steeped in conducting himself like that."

Charles E. Potter, Jr., Journalist
August 12, 2000
The New London Day

"Sen. Lieberman is a Jew. But he is also a man, an American, a political leader, and one of the most respected men in Connecticut, in Congress and in the country. The only valid question for voters is Lieberman's ability to manage the office of vice president and, if the need arises, to assume the presidency.

"That Lieberman is a Jew is inconsequential."

Reverend Edward C. Martin
August 12, 2000
The Los Angeles Times

"He has unquestionable credentials to serve as vice president or even president of the United States. No one has challenged that. Instead, the questions swirl around his religion."

William F. Buckley, Jr., Columnist
and Founder of The National Review
August 12, 2000
The Houston Chronicle

"Joseph Lieberman is many things, besides being Jewish. He is enormously talented as a human being and as a friend."

Richard Benedetto, Columnist
August 12, 2000
USA Today

"[Lieberman] is viewed by most analysts as a ploy to blunt GOP attempts to link Gore to Clinton on the moral question."

Alan Abelson, Columnist
August 14, 2000
Barron's

"Mr. Lieberman, instead of bringing the customary invisible presence (or at least visible only to the extent of an occasional glimpse grinning foolishly over the presidential candidate's right shoulder), is burdened with endowing the campaign with gravitas."

APPENDIX III

Selected Statements by Senator Lieberman

Armed Services

*From Opening Address before the U.S. Army Conference on
    Strategic Responsiveness*
November 2, 1999

"In the process of military transformation, there will be
winners and losers. We will need to disinvest in programs that
have great bureaucratic and political power. And we will have
to change beliefs that lie at the core of great organizations, and
that will be resisted by some. We can take some comfort in the
fact that this is not the first revolution in military affairs and
others have successfully managed this challenge in the past.
And we will too. It is our turn now and our responsibility to go
forward. As Sir Francis Bacon said centuries ago, 'He who will
not apply new remedies must expect new evils.' "

Budget

*On "Fiscal Discipline" Amendment to Strike Entire $792
    Billion Republican Tax Bill*
July 28, 1999

"For the American economy, and for millions of American
families, these are truly the best of times. Growth is high, un-

employment is low, the stock market is surprisingly high, and inflation is surprisingly low.

"It took a lot of hard work by a lot of people to get to this plentiful place. The Federal Government helped create the climate for sustained economic growth by exercising some real fiscal discipline, but most of the prosperity has come—as it always does in America—from the private sector, from millions of businesses and workers innovating, cooperating, and profiting.

"And now, as a result, for the first time in a generation, the Federal Government's books appear to show a surplus, with some even predicting that we will be a trillion dollars in the black over the next decade. We have achieved fiscal stability. We are well positioned for economic security. And before the ink is barely dry on the projections, I am afraid, we are about to jeopardize it all.

"Oscar Wilde once wrote: 'I can resist everything except temptation.' The same may well be said of this Congress, as it proceeds merrily to spend a surplus that no one knows is really there, to take our nation back into deficit before we could even appreciate the projection of a surplus, and endanger the critical economic gains we have made over the past several years.

"Why not stay the course that has raised the standard of living of millions of American families for at least another year? Why not wait to see if the surplus projections are real, if the economy will continue to grow, if Congress is prepared to exercise the required spending discipline?

"That's the question I will ask my colleagues in the Senate as we begin debate today on the $792 billion Republican tax bill. It is my intention to offer an amendment that would postpone any surplus-based tax cuts at this time. It does not make use of triggers or any other gimmicks or conditions. Instead it simply strikes out the entire body of the Republican bill. In doing so, it would shut down debate on tax cuts for the immediate future, and thus allow for more thought and consideration over how best to proceed in the years ahead, as the surplus hopefully becomes less of a projection and more of a tangible, calculable asset.

"Arriving at this position was not easy for me. As a New Democrat, an adherent of the rising-tide-lifts-all-boats philosophy, and a long-time proponent of reducing taxes, my reflex is to propose tax cuts, not to oppose them. I would welcome the opportunity to vote for a balanced, thoughtfully crafted tax reduction package—if we could afford it, and if the economy needed it.

"But the more I have studied the budgetary assumptions we are using, the more I have concluded we are probably facing a 'potemkin' surplus, not a real one, and therefore it is too soon to presume that we can afford the hundreds of billions of dollars in tax cuts being proposed.

"The reality is that the baselines that CBO and OMB are using assume that we will grow at an annual average rate of 2.4 percent for the next 10 years, which is to say that they assume that the longest peacetime expansion in our history will continue uninterrupted for another decade. This could happen, but it would mean the end of the business cycle as we have known it, and that the U.S. economy would be immune to the volatile forces of the increasingly interconnected global economy. Again, this is possible, but I would not bank on it, or at least I would not spend the profits of such unprecedented projected growth until I knew they were in the bank.

"Both baselines also assume politically untenable discretionary spending levels. For a $1 trillion on-budget surplus to materialize, Congress must keep discretionary spending under existing caps through 2002 and then only adjusted for inflation through 2009. This will result in massive cuts in domestic discretionary and defense spending, as much as $786 billion over the next 10 years under the Republican plan. These are cuts that few in either house would ever support, and, in fact, are not supporting right now, as Congress today simply exceeds the budget caps through transparent accounting games, calling any excess spending emergency spending and double-counting when helpful.

"In other words, we don't have to wonder whether Congress will be able to hold the spending line on which the surplus is contingent over the next decade, because Congress is already proving today it cannot so control itself.

"The Concord Coalition has turned out an insightful budget analysis that underscores what would happen if we work from more realistic baselines.

"For example, if we presume that discretionary spending will simply grow with inflation from 2000 through 2009, which is about half of the rate it has grown in the last decade, and that we will continue to make emergency appropriations at current rates, our on-budget surplus would only be $46 billion dollars ten years from now, not $1 trillion. That is a good $200 billion less than the smallest tax cut being proposed.

"The result is that by passing a major tax cut, one paid for with what may be an imaginary surplus, we would likely incur sizable deficits for years to come. That would add more to our mountainous debt, send a troubling signal to the financial markets about our fiscal responsibility, and probably throttle back our economy. On top of that, we would leave little or no money available for building the solvency of Medicare and Social Security, and thus raise the specter of a major tax increase down the line to compensate for our profligacy now.

"Finally, I was ultimately persuaded by the case Alan Greenspan recently made against a passing a major tax cut at this moment, particularly one that would be skewed toward reducing personal income taxes, when the economy is humming, and in, Chairman Greenspan's view, in danger of inflating.

"It seems quite clear from Chairman Greenspan that if we cut taxes now, he will increase interest rates soon after. This would put a drag on the economy, slowing down business investment, stunting our prospects for growth, and probably lowering the stock market. It would also hit average working Americans literally where they live—driving up the cost of their mortgages, car payments, credit card bills, and student loans—to the point that it could well dwarf any tax benefit they would receive from Congress. In other words, we would be robbing Peter to pay Paul, while simultaneously robbing our economy of the dynamism we have labored so hard to create.

"For what purpose? No one argues that the economy needs a tax cut now. What we need now, I would argue, is a healthy dose of fiscal willpower. So our call today is to put the brakes on the headlong rush to cut taxes before we spend what is now just the suggestion of a surplus, and to show some more of the fiscal discipline and responsibility that was critical to generating the economic growth we are enjoying today."

Encouraging Passage of Biennial Budget and Appropriations Act
February 2, 2000

"I am proud to be a co-sponsor of S. 92, the Biennial Budget and Appropriations Act, and I thank my colleagues here today for all their work in pushing this bill forward. This legislation would bring more order and stability to Congress, by alleviating the gridlock so often caused by our annual confrontations over budget and appropriations.

"The Congressional Research Service has reported that between ½ and ¾ of Congress's time is spent on budget and appropriation votes. In 1996, 73 percent of the votes the Senate took were related to the budget. And over the last 50 years, Congress has only twice met the deadline for passing all thirteen appropriations bills. Yet, according to a CBO analysis, 96% of our spending on discretionary accounts is predictable. In other words, the grinding annual budget and appropriations cycle is taking up far too much of Congress' time, for no good reason.

"The annual budget and appropriations process is not just time consuming, it can be chaotic and haphazard, especially towards the end of the fiscal year, when the parties will often engage in a showdown in an attempt to win last minute concessions. Our citizens expect more from their government, and we can all sense their disaffection with the gridlock that has so often gripped this place. Moving to a two year cycle may not completely eliminate this problem, but it will help a great deal. Not only will our bill give Congress more time to legislate and engage in oversight, it also provides more time to work through the budget and appropriations process in an orderly fashion. And those of our constituents who are alienated from their government need to see that we can address the nation's business in a systematic and orderly way."

Campaign Finance Reform

Regarding the Introduction of the McCain-Feingold Campaign Finance Reform Legislation into the 106th Congress
January 19, 1999

"Campaign finance reformers have had a tough time overcoming Senate filibusters in the past few years but we will weather on until we pass this bill. Ultimately, the free flow of soft money in our election system will be recognized as the corrupt practice it is by at least 60 Senators.

"Our country has experienced a crisis of confidence in its political leaders lately. What better way to start restoring the people's faith in elected representatives than by approving campaign finance reform?"

Consumer Affairs

Regarding the Deceptive Mail Prevention and Enforcement Act
August 2, 1999

"These days, sweepstakes mailings often involve sophisticated marketing techniques that persuade recipients to spend money in hopes of finding the pot of gold at the end of the rainbow. But sweepstakes companies are in business to sell products and make profits. Plain and simple. That's legitimate, as long as they do it fairly and truthfully.

"I strongly support this legislation as a tool to help consumers negotiate their way through the high-pressure sales tactics sometimes employed by marketers in this highly competitive age."

*Praising FCC/FTC Action to Protect Consumers of Long
    Distance Telephone Services*
March 1, 2000

"With vigorous competition thriving in the long distance market, companies will increasingly rely upon advertising to gain customers. The policy announced today will help ensure that this advertising is fair and accurate. This means that the ads may provide only truthful, substantiated statements with clear and conspicuous disclosure of material facts. Companies that try to obtain consumers' business by misleading them about their prices and services will have to answer to these regulators.

"Long-distance telephone service has become a necessity in today's society where family and friends are often spread out in several states and the only link with an elderly parent or a sick friend is the telephone. Disclosure and pricing rules like these are vital to consumers in making informed decisions about their long-distance carriers."

Regarding Consumer Health Information on the Internet
May 24, 2000

"The Internet has tremendous potential as a tool to help consumers manage their own health care, and, in fact, Americans are flocking to health care sites to take advantage of that potential. Important as this information is for the health of American consumers, it is not always reliable—and that's why we are here today: to try and ensure that consumers receive the facts that will help them assess the value of the medical information they are getting. So how can consumers tell what information is reliable and what criteria to use to determine reliability? Organizations like the eHealth Ethics Initiative (which is releasing its ethical code here today) and others are trying to provide the tools consumers need to make their own informed choices. I applaud that.

"But issuing a code of ethics is only a beginning, as the eHealth Ethics people will readily acknowledge. The next step is to encourage online health sites to comply with a code, verify that they do comply, and then educate consumers on how to use this new tool.

"To move us down that road, I have drafted a bill—which I expect to introduce shortly. My goal is not to impose federal standards on the Internet in any way but rather to lend government's support to industry self-regulation. My bill would require the chairman of the Federal Trade Commission and the secretaries of Health and Human Services and Veterans Affairs to review the proposed codes. If they do not adequately serve consumers, a committee of private and public sector representatives would work to set better standards, enforce and publicize them."

Contract with America

On the Occasion of His Assuming the DLC Chairmanship
March 1, 1995

"The Contract with America has few genuinely new ideas and was packaged more by poll and focus group than by visionaries designing a novel approach to leadership. There is very little in it for those tens of millions of Americans who ask themselves, 'How am I going to send my kid to college . . . prepare for retirement . . . find a new job when I get laid off . . . be sure my health insurance won't be taken away . . . and protect my family from crime?' "

Economics

On Women's Business Center Program
November 4, 1999

"Women entrepreneurs are increasingly crucial to our national prosperity, and in a short time, Connecticut's centers have already produced a number of success stories. Part of good government is knowing which programs work and which ones don't. When you identify one that works as well as the Women's Business Center program, you nurture it, which is precisely what this bill seeks to do."

Before Congress
Introducing the Savings for Working Families Act of 2000
February 2, 2000

"The stock market is jumping to record highs, inflation and unemployment are hovering at record lows, and millions of Americans are reaping the benefit, including millions of middle-class families. But millions more are clearly not, with studies showing that incomes for many low-income households are declining relative to the wealthiest Americans, and the gulf between the have-mosts and the have-leasts is widening as a result.

"The Savings for Working Families Act that Senators Santorum and I, along with Senators Abraham, Feinstein, Landrieu, and Bayh, are introducing today might just offer a bipartisan model for getting us there. It brings together Democrats and Republicans, policy wonks and working moms, and even bankers and consumers, all in support of a new approach to sustaining some old American ideals—rewarding work, encouraging responsibility, and expanding opportunity.

"We spell this new idea IDA, which stands for Individual Development Accounts. Banks and credit unions and other community organizations that offer these special accounts match deposits dollar-for-dollar to encourage workers to save for the future, and in return workers commit to use the proceeds to buy a home, upgrade their education or start a business. Why this limitation? Because assets matter. As most experts will attest, success in today's economy increasingly is defined by asset ownership, and while millions of Americans are tapped into the bull market, many more are simply tapped out, with few assets to speak of, and therefore little hope of accumulating the means for upward mobility and real security."

Education

At the DLC Annual Conference
January 27, 1997

"Our public schools are crumbling inside and out, and we must ask ourselves why. One reason I believe we have allowed this to happen is that somehow over the years the word 'standards' became unfashionable and unacceptable. But is it a wrong 'standard' for our kids to have a schoolhouse with a roof that is not crumbling and other students who don't threaten them?

"Is it wrong for good teachers to want to break free from stultifying bureaucracies so they can better teach our kids? Is it wrong for our parents to have a choice among schools, so that their kids can get the best education possible? Is it wrong for our kids to be denied national education standards so we can know better how they're doing and they can better compete for the college of their choice and the career of their choice?

"It is not wrong. It is a right. And that is why we need to right the wrongs of our system of education."

Regarding the Public Education Reinvestment, Reinvention,
*   and Responsibility Act*
November 16, 1999

"We as New Democrats believe there is a better way, a third way, that synthesizes the best ideas of both sides into a progressive, practical blueprint for real change. A way to reinvent our public education system without retreating from our common commitment to the common school. A way to refocus our priorities to help every child in every state learn at a high level. And ultimately a way to restore public faith in our public schools.

"Making this a viable successor to the existing ESEA won't be easy; we are proposing some dramatic changes that will shake up the status quo and its defenders. But we are encouraged by the fact that Governor Bush of Texas has proposed a reform plan that is remarkably similar to our proposal, which suggests that maybe we are closer to breaking the education stalemate than some may think and to achieving a true consensus on how to revitalize our public schools."

Regarding the Cost of College Tuition
February 9, 2000

"The high price of a college education is an issue of growing concern for American families. Over the past twenty years, tuition has more than doubled at both public and private schools. Yet, subsidies to schools, in the form of state appropriations, as well as aid to students and their families, have failed to keep pace with those cost increases.

"Parents seem to be willing to shoulder almost any burden to give their children the help they need, but when they hear the College Board reporting that 'four-year college tuitions increased an average of more than 110 percent over inflation' since the early '80s, they fear that the burden is increasing to back-breaking proportions, and that their children will be priced out of the market.

"The stress on individual students and families is only part of the story. There is also a powerful connection between our nation's ability to provide higher education and its ability to maintain healthy economic growth. We regularly hear from employers about America's shortage of skilled workers necessary to help them compete globally. If college becomes a luxury that an increasing percentage of our population cannot afford, the economic divide between higher education "haves" and "have-nots" will widen to the point where it undercuts the American dream and stunts our economic growth."

On Charter Schools
February 11, 2000

"This report documents statistically what we have been hearing anecdotally for the last several years—that charter schools are working and realizing a hopeful vision of the future of public education.

"The best evidence of that is the fact that a growing legion of educators, businessmen, parents and community leaders are not just talking about education reform but taking it into their own hands by starting charters, and the fact that a growing legion of parents are affirmatively choosing to entrust their children to these independent, innovative places of learning.

"It is a testament to the appeal and success of the charter model that it has generated strong bipartisan support across the country and here in Congress, which was evident in the unanimous passage of the Charter School Expansion Act two years ago.

"President Clinton's vision and leadership have been particularly important to the growth of the charter school movement. He was an early advocate of charters as a way of injecting more choice, flexibility and accountability into our public school system, and he has continually pushed for more federal support. I look forward to working with him and my colleagues here in Congress to build on the successful work being done in communities across the country."

*Regarding House-Senate Resolution on American History
    Education*
June 27, 2000

"When we lose the memory of our past, when we lose our understanding of the remarkable individuals, events, and values that have shaped this nation, we are losing much of what it means to be an American. We are losing touch with the civic glue that binds our diverse nation into a single people with a common purpose. And, I fear, we are losing sight of the lessons our history teaches us and the fundamental responsibilities we share as citizens in a free democracy.

"We have come together today to call attention to this national problem and hopefully begin mobilizing a national response. In that spirit, we will introduce resolutions in the House and Senate expressing our common concern in advance of the July 4th holiday. We want to take this moment of patriotism to reaffirm the value we place on our truly exceptional history and make an appeal to begin work immediately on rebuilding our historical literacy."

Energy

Before Congress
At the Oversight Hearing on Rising Oil Prices
March 23, 2000

"I have made plain my view that the first response to the oil crunch would be for the administration to draw down from the Strategic Petroleum Reserve to add to supply that will reduce prices. This year's oil price increases have been so extreme that consumers and businesses are feeling the effects across the board: increasing inflation and the likelihood of further hikes in interest rates. I remain concerned that the administration has not taken any steps to tap the reserve, but I am cheered that some of our witnesses advocate this approach, or alternately, a swap that would involve the release of reserve oil now to refiners, in exchange for a promise to return additional amounts of oil to the reserve in future. This plan would lower oil prices by increasing oil supply in the SPR.

"But if we step back and look at the big picture, it's easy to see this price volatility and the threat it presents as a symptom of a deeper, more long-term problem: our dependence on foreign oil. By failing to provide our own citizens with energy alternatives, we limit our options in times of national emergencies and entrust our economic security to the whims of others. It is imperative that we take concrete steps to wean ourselves from foreign oil and develop a domestic infrastructure to deliver reliable alternatives. First, we need to invest time, money, and energy in increasing our domestic gas and oil production, and diversifying our energy mix to include more solar energy, fuel cells, wind, and nuclear power, and developing long-range strategies for harnessing these additional energy sources.

"Second, in the context of the utility deregulation debate, Senator Jeffords and I are cosponsoring legislation, the Clean Energy Act, that would require utilities to use renewables for 2.5 percent of their power in 2000 and 20 percent by the year 2020. We intend to offer this plan as an amendment to any deregulation bill that comes before the Senate. I am happy to announce that last month, the Senate passed another bill that Senators Jeffords and I cosponsored, the National Sustainable Fuels and Chemicals Act, which creates a bold R&D project to produce fuels from plants and crop biomass. This legislation can significantly increase the viability of domestic sources of renewable energy.

"Third, we must take stock of the domestic energy market and evaluate national and individual consumer decisions affecting our own energy supply and efficiency. In some areas the results are encouraging. Conservation measures taken by U.S. businesses have significantly improved the efficiency of the overall economy. During the crisis of the 1970s, nearly nine percent of our GDP was spent on oil. That is down to three percent today. We can and should build on this progress.

"The outlook is not so bright across all sectors of the economy. Consider our driving habits. Over the last 30 years, vehicle miles traveled have increased by 130 percent. And despite early improvements in fuel efficiency, current standards have stagnated and Congress has imposed a "freeze" on raising—or even studying the benefits of raising—corporate average fuel efficiency.

"I cannot state strongly enough the need to enhance our nation's fuel efficiency—to conserve the resources that we do have and to reduce our dependence on foreign suppliers—for the sake of a stronger economy and a cleaner environment.

"Finally, it is critical that we rule out what are not viable solutions, such as opening up protected spaces for domestic oil drilling. Some have once again suggested that we target the Arctic National Wildlife Refuge as a suitable spot for drilling.

The U.S. Geological Survey estimates there are 3.2 billion barrels, or less than a six-month supply, of commercially recoverable oil in the ANWR. This means the refuge would never meet more than two percent of our nation's needs at any given time. The answer to our foreign oil dependency is not to drill in and damage our national treasures but to look to increasing our own energy efficiency and finding alternative and renewable sources of energy.

"I hope we can use this moment of dwindling oil supply and rising prices to heed the warning signs, to think about our future health and security as a nation, and to enact a new progressive energy policy for this new century."

Environment

On Protecting the Arctic National Wildlife Refuge
April 22, 1999

"The coastal plain of the Arctic Refuge is home to the wildest and most pristine arctic coastal ecosystem in the United States. It is the place where the calves of the awe-inspiring Porcupine caribou herd are born every year, where snow geese feed in the fall, where many female polar bears choose to den, and where red-throated loons, American golden-plovers, and many other important migratory birds flock to each summer.

"This is, in short, a national treasure, a measure of God's majesty, and we have an obligation as the stewards of the earth today to protect it for our children and generations to come. On this Earth Day, we are rededicating ourselves to that important mission and the fundamental value we as Americans place on the conservation of our great natural resources."

Regarding the National Resources Reinvestment Act of 1999
August 16, 1999

"Because I'm committed to preserving a rich environmental legacy for our children, when I return to Washington in September, I will introduce the Natural Resources Reinvestment Act of 1999 with Senator Chafee, from Rhode Island, the Chairman of the Environment and Public Works Committee on which I serve, and Senators Leahy and Jeffords, from Vermont.

"The principle behind the bill is simple: as we deplete federally-owned, non-renewable natural resources such as oil and gas, we should reinvest the proceeds to establish a reliable source of funding for state, local, and federal efforts to conserve land and water, provide recreational opportunities, preserve historic resources, protect fish and wildlife, and preserve open space. The Natural Resources Reinvestment Act honors this principle by re-establishing America's long-standing commitment to protecting land, fish and wildlife, and our cultural heritage and by re-doubling federal commitments that help states and localities protect the open space and recreational opportunities that Americans cherish so deeply."

On New Emissions Standards
December 22, 1999

"When Congress passed the Clean Air Act Amendments of 1990, none of us anticipated how the demand for sport utility vehicles and light trucks would soar. The number of larger, light duty personal vehicles on the road has doubled since 1970, and the number of miles Americans are traveling each year has doubled over this time period, as well. Until today, the emission standard for these larger cars has been two to five times lower than for passenger cars, leading to higher levels of ozone and particulates that decrease lung function and cause respiratory problems like asthma. Under today's proposal, for the first time, these vehicles will have to meet the same protective standards as other passenger vehicles.

"The new proposal will help us all breathe easier, while helping to pave the way for the low and ultra-low emissions vehicles of the future."

On Global Warming
January 12, 2000

"Naysayers have spent years suggesting that satellite data would disprove the existence of global climate change. The NAS report shows that just the opposite is true, that in fact surface temperatures are rising even faster than originally predicted, and well above the average of the previous 100 years.

"To continue to ignore this evidence is truly to live with our heads in the clouds, and in a state of denial comparable to the flat earth fanatics. Global warming is happening, as the NAS attests, and could have potentially disastrous consequences for our children and our grandchildren if we do not take it seriously.

"We must make a strong commitment to reduce our emissions of greenhouse gases, and a good place to start would be to fund the President's request for energy efficiency and research programs for clean and renewable energy. I hope the Academy's findings will build support for this modest downpayment, and summon the leadership necessary to take on this critical challenge."

Regarding House Bill to Revitalize Long Island Sound
May 9, 2000

"Over the past ten years, the states of Connecticut and New York, advocacy groups, residents, tradesmen, and scientists have all devoted significant time and attention to develop a plan to make the Sound sound once again. They have also devoted significant resources as well—New York State has approved $200 million for Long Island Sound as part of a $1.75 billion bond act, and Connecticut has awarded more than $200 million in the past three years to support upgrades at sewage treatment plants.

"The EPA's Long Island Sound Office has been given the daunting challenge of orchestrating this multibillion dollar clean-up effort and the many partners participating in it, who

are all working toward reducing the damaging nitrogen load-
ings that degrade the Sound's water quality and rescuing the
habitats that help feed our regional economy. The Sound Office
has made great progress with limited means, but if we want to
realize our ultimate goals, then we must step up our support at
the federal level.

"Last September, I introduced legislation in the Senate
with my colleagues from Connecticut and New York that aims
to fulfill that critical commitment. Our bill would reauthorize
the EPA's Long Island Sound Office for five years and, most
importantly, increase its funding for cooperative grants to $10
million, which would leverage additional state and local resources and significantly expand the constructive work that is
already being done.

"That legislation, S. 1632, passed the Senate Environment
and Public Works Committee unanimously on October 13th,
and now awaits floor action. I am grateful that the House Water
Resources and Environment Subcommittee has agreed today to
consider a companion bill sponsored by Representatives Johnson and Lazio, the Long Island Sound Restoration Act, and I
look forward to working with my colleagues from Connecticut
and New York to meet this pressing need this year."

Foreign Policy

Regarding Ethnic Massacre in Kosovo
January 19, 1999

"The credibility of the United States and NATO is at stake
here. We must act forcefully. Unless Milosevic immediately
comes into compliance with the cease-fire agreement by return-
ing his troops to barracks and drastically lowering the number
of police operating in Kosovo, NATO, under the leadership of
the United States, should take military action to force the Serbs
to abide by the agreement. NATO cannot allow one man to
destabilize a key region in Europe."

On the Kosovo Self Defense Act of 1999
March 25, 1999

"I am proud to join with Senator McConnell today in proposing the Kosovo Self Defense Act of 1999, legislation that would provide funding to help arm and train the Kosovars to repel further aggression by the Yugoslav forces.

"In putting forward this plan, I want to say that I hope it never needs to be implemented. I hope we never need to appropriate the money we would authorize with this bill. Indeed, I hope Slobodan Milosevic soon realizes that it would be in his and the Serbian people's best interests to accept the Rambouillet Agreement and end the violence in Serbia. All the people in Serbia deserve the promise of peace and a chance to rebuild their lives and their communities.

"However, if, after extended air strikes, it becomes clear that Milosevic intends to continue his war of aggression against the Kosovar people, we must have an answer to the question of what next—not just for the protection of our national interests and our credibility, not just for the protection of our men and women in harm's way, but for the protection of those Kosovars who we know Milosevic will continue to slaughter if this conflict drags on. The bill we are proposing provides us with such an answer, and an opportunity to send an uncompromising message to Milosevic: we will not stand idly by and allow Milosevic to brutalize the people of Kosovo any longer.

"This bill is premised on our belief that NATO ground forces—including American troops—will not be put into Kosovo unless the Serbs and Kosovars reach a peace agreement. If we adopt that stance, though, and Serbian aggression continues, we have an obligation to allow the Kosovars to defend themselves. Our legislation, by providing aid to the Kosovar military forces, would give them a fair chance to fight for their families and their future.

"I am aware that this proposal will raise some concerns. I recall that when Senator Dole and I first raised the idea of training and equipping the Bosnian Army, many critics told us that we would destabilize an entire region or accelerate an arms race. In the end, I think those concerns were shown to be misguided. Training and equipping the Bosnians created a balance of power that enhanced the stability of the area and helped end the Bosnian war.

"I realize that the situation in Kosovo is different. But that difference does not diminish the suffering of the Kosovar people subject to Serb aggression, nor negate their right to defend their families from the threat of genocide.

"The proposal we put forward today clarifies the choice Milosevic must make. He can sign Rambouillet, which would mean the Kosovars would disarm and the conflict would end. Or he can continue to resist all reason by refusing to sign and continue his aggression and genocide. If he chooses the second option, he must realize that, rather than disarming the Kosovars, we will train and equip them so they can fight. Those are his choices. Let us hope and pray he makes the right choice."

Before Congress
On Cosponsoring a Senate Resolution Authorizing the Use of
    "All Necessary Force" in Kosovo
April 20, 1999

"Great nations such as this one and great alliances such as NATO do not remain great if they do not uphold their principles and keep their promises. That has always been true, of course, but it seems powerfully so today, in this city, as we prepare to welcome NATO and much of the rest of the world to Washington this week to commemorate the 50th anniversary of this great alliance.

"We are being tested, both this alliance and this nation, in ways that a few months ago we would never have imagined would have been the case as we prepared for this commemoration. So it becomes in its way less an unlimited celebration and more a renewal of commitment to the principles that animated and necessitated the organization of NATO 50 years ago.

"We're called on today to uphold those principles, the principles of a free and secure transatlantic community. And we must keep the promises that we have made in support of those principles. NATO must prevail in the Balkans, in Kosovo. Thugs, renegade regimes and power hungry maniacs everywhere in the world are watching our actions in the Balkans and gauging our resolve. They must receive an unequivocal message. They must understand that they violate our principles, that they ignore our promises and threats at their peril."

On the Sudan Peace Act
July 27, 1999

"I am proud to join with Senators Frist and Brownback today in introducing the Sudan Peace Act, a bill that aims to facilitate the pursuit of peace in this war-torn African nation, to stop the ongoing brutalization of the Sudanese people, particularly its Christian citizens, and, on a larger plane, to affirm that our concerns for human rights and our commitment to democratic values transcend continental boundaries.

"Over the last 15 years, at least 2 million people in Sudan have died, while another 4 million have been forced to leave their homes. This is a conservative estimate, with the true death toll remaining both unknown and unknowable. The exact number is not critical, though, for no single statistic could begin to convey the depth of the suffering or the horror of the atrocities the Sudanese people have been experiencing, from widescale enslavement to mass murder to the government's systematic use of famine as a weapon of mass destruction.

"Sudan's tragedy is fast becoming our test. We just went to war to stop a similarly repulsive campaign of repression in Kosovo, and our non-intervention in the Sudan has led some to question the consistency with which we apply our core democratic values and act on our humanitarian impulses.

"In responding to these questions, we have to be clear that the Sudan is not Kosovo. Our vital interests are not threatened there, nor is the stability of Europe, the crucible of two world wars and the home to our closest allies, or the credibility of NATO itself, our primary international alliance.

"But at the same time, we also have to be clear that to make this distinction is not to distance ourselves from the assault on our shared humanitarian and political values occurring in Sudan, or from our moral obligation to do what we reasonably can to free the Sudanese people from this onslaught of oppression.

"The legislation we are introducing today is an effort to fulfill that obligation, to bring the weight of our conscience to bear and push the combatants in Sudan to reach a comprehensive, negotiated, and principled peace. It would tap a host of levers—from tightening sanctions to reforming the delivery of humanitarian aid to calling for human rights monitors in trouble spots—to significantly step up the pressure on the government to work out a settlement that ends the bloodshed.

"We cannot hold out any guarantees of success. But we can hold up our common values of democracy, political and religious freedom, and human rights, much as we did in Kosovo, and make an unequivocal statement about America's moral leadership in the world, which is why this legislation could and would make a difference, and why I hope it will soon be enacted."

Before Congress
Regarding the Comprehensive Test Ban Treaty
October 12, 1999

"Let's keep the hope of a more secure world alive. Let's acknowledge that we have a common goal. Is anybody for nuclear proliferation? Don't we all agree that the atmosphere is cleaner and the likelihood of nuclear proliferation less if nations can't test? Can't we find a way across party lines to do what we have done with other treaties to adopt reservations or safeguards or conditions which allow enough of us to come together to ratify this treaty? Why are we heading toward a wall from which there will be no good return and no good result?"

Before Congress
In Support of the Iran Nonproliferation Act
February 22, 2000

"So the focus of our concern about Iran, the fact that it has been our most implacable foe in the recent past, that it has been the single most intransigent supporter of terrorism against this nation and our allies, that remains, unfortunately, in reality still unchanged. And the thought that weapons of mass destruction carried by ballistic missiles would be in the possession of this nation, still controlled effectively by this small group of enemies of the United States should fill us with the most profound fear and anxiety. And it is from that fear and anxiety that this bill emerges.

"This is not the first time that we have expressed our concerns about these developments in Iran. In previous enactments we have given the Administration the tools to try to address this problem, specifically in the Arms Export Control Act and in the Iran Iraq Sanctions Act. But we weren't satisfied with those and the way they were being used, so we passed the Iran Missile Proliferations Sanction Act in 1997, a measure similar to this legislation that we're considering today. Unfortunately the President chose to veto that legislation, and that is why HR 1883 was introduced, why it passed the House overwhelmingly, 419 to 0. with every Member of both parties supporting it. Since then, our concern about the problem, that since 1997 has not diminished. It is widely and reliably reported, and that is why we are back with this legislation, that entities and people in Russia continue to provide both technology and assistance to Iran to build these dangerous weapons, and Iran has made worrying progress on its missile program as the Majority Leader indicated, and as the intelligence, classified as it is, which is available to our colleagues clearly state.

"These programs in Iran can profoundly change the balance of power in the region, and strike a very serious blow to our effort to contain Iran until it becomes a responsible member of the community of nations, until the forces of change which are blowing so hopefully through Iran even as we speak here today, reach fruition and a change of policy. I'm sure most everyone in this chamber would look forward to a day hopefully when sanctions of this kind would not be necessary because a new government representing what seems to be a clear will of the Iranian people would be in power in Tehran, with the government which the United States of America and our allies could have constructive and peaceful relations. But until that time, the kinds of weapons that are being developed would allow Iran to threaten friendly Arab states, for instance, making it harder for them to cooperate with the United States. They would raise the risks to U.S. military forces in the region, and would threaten the free flow of oil in this critical region, which could create crises in places far from the Persian Gulf.

"We must act to try to prevent this from happening. It seems to me self-evident and axiomatic that we have to do whatever we can to try to delay and retard this dangerous capability, given the Iranian government that exists now. Part of that is making clear, in no uncertain terms, that the time for assistance to Iran for the development of these dangerous weapons is over. In addition to other sanctions, we have focused in this bill on holding up so-called "extraordinary" U.S. funding to the Russian Space Agency for the International Space Station unless Russia takes sufficient action to halt proliferation to Iran.

"This is our attempt to demonstrate the seriousness of our concern about this matter, even to the extent of stopping the funding of a program—space cooperation—that is not only important to us, but important to the Russians. While we cannot expect to prevent all technology transfers to rogue states, we do have the ability to check the flow of some of it by adopting the sanctions aimed at those engaged in such activity. We must act to take measures against those governments that condone such activity, whether or not they are organizing and abetting the transfer, or merely looking the other way when their citizens engage in these activities."

Gun Control

Before Congress
Regarding "Safe Havens" Gun Safety Resolution
April 14, 2000

"Ask any parent, educator, and congregant, and they'll say every community is entitled to at least a few sites of sanctuary, where they can honor their families and their God without fearing for their safety or their lives. But the reality is that at least 22 states permit gun owners to carry concealed weapons in places of worship, and many allow them at school events off campus.

"Why does anyone other than a law enforcement officer need to carry a firearm into these public spaces? Why at this moment of such concern about gun violence do we want to add to it and the potential for more terror and tragedy in what should be our safest places? Why after at least a dozen shootings in American churches and synagogues over the last five years do we want to invite another?

"Repealing these exceptions for concealed weapons would put the law on the right side of reason. It would help diminish the odds that another Columbine is around the corner. And it would reassure the American people that it is possible for us to come together on common ground to fight this threat to our safety and security.

"This in the end is not an ideological or constitutional issue, but a question of common sense. We can respect the rights of hunters and legitimate gun owners while also acknowledging that bullets and Bibles don't mix. This is not a hard line to take. Nor should it be a hard line to draw, in order to provide our safe havens for our families."

Healthcare

Before Congress
In Support of a Women's Health Care Amendment to the
Patients' Bill of Rights in the Senate
July 13, 1999

"Along with most women and most Americans, I believe that a woman should have the choice and the freedom to select an OB/GYN physician as her primary care provider and to determine, in consultation with her doctor, how long she should stay in the hospital following surgery.

"Those critical and deeply personal judgments should not be trumped by the arbitrary guidelines of managed care companies. The women in our lives deserve better than drive-by mastectomies. With this amendment, we will say so in law, and ensure that women receive the services they need and the respect they are owed."

Before Congress
Introducing the SAFE Act
April 6, 2000

"The SAFE Act picks up on the leading recommendations of the Institute of Medicine and President Clinton. The President and IOM deserve credit for recognizing that errors are preventable and praise for recommending specific steps to immunize our medical system from mistakes. I hope our presence here today is proof that their work will be acted upon. After all, we are all patients at one time or another, and want to be so in the safest system possible.

"As I prepared this legislation, my thoughts returned to 1965, the year consumer advocate and Connecticut resident Ralph Nader wrote a book called *Unsafe at Any Speed*. Mr. Nader began his work on highway safety as a consultant under then-Secretary of Labor Daniel Patrick Moynihan in 1964. Many of the shocking findings in *Unsafe at Any Speed* were gathered by Mr. Nader while preparing a government study for Secretary Moynihan. Both the report and the book transformed our perceptions of safety in the automobile industry and led to dramatic changes that have saved countless lives on the highway and on neighborhood streets.

"The IOM's report, "To Err is Human," can have the same impact on safety within the health care system. Like Ralph Nader thirty-five years ago, the IOM has focused the nation's attention on thousands of preventable deaths and injuries. If we can persuade the health care industry to follow the example of the automobile industry, thirty-five years from now, hospitals, nursing homes, and other health care facilities will be much safer places.

"No one should have to worry about the quality of their health care more than they do about their drive home."

Leadership

Before the Democratic Leadership Council
On the Occasion of His Assuming the DLC Chairmanship
March 1, 1995

"Back in 1962, I had the honor of being in an audience in New Haven, Connecticut, when President John F. Kennedy said these words: 'Too often we hold fast to the cliches of our forebears . . . we enjoy the comfort of opinion without the discomfort of thought.'

"That sums up for me the dilemma of American politics today. Many members of both parties have not given enough thought to the significance of the fundamental changes that are occurring in our country. As a result, people are disillusioned, alienated, and frustrated. Their elected leaders are talking about all sorts of things except what is important to them, such as the fact that three out of five Americans are making fewer real dollars than they did 15 years ago. That is a startling reversal of fortune. It is the stuff of which revolutions are made."

To The National Press Club
March 9, 1995

"Do we remain on the old, worn roads of comfortable partisanship and ideology . . . or do we set out in a whole new direction toward a third way, where the concerns of the people are met with fresh, common-sense ideas? I believe that charting a new course represents the best choice for our party and for our nation. And I believe the DLC can be the beacon of light our nation and our party needs to guide us along the path to a progressive future."

Supporting the "Building Livable Communities" Initiative
     announced by Vice President Gore
January 11, 1999

"How the Federal Government helps to develop and re-develop the American landscape for the 21st Century isn't a luxury. It's a great opportunity, a human necessity, and fiscal responsibility that will build a better Connecticut and a better America.

"This initiative is a down payment for the future. It's about being smart so that our kids in the 21st Century can avoid some the environmental, transportation, and housing mistakes we've made in the 20th Century. It's about being responsible and inclusive. Livability does not stop at town lines or state borders. This initiative recognizes that reality and builds solutions into the Federal Budget. I am proud to support that effort."

Media and Entertainment

Before Congress
Upon Joining the Center for Media and Public Affairs in
     Releasing Report on "Merchandising Mayhem"
September 22, 1999

"According to the CMPA, the 500-plus music videos, television series, and major motion pictures they evaluated averaged one scene of Media Violence Study serious violence every four minutes—for a two hour movie, that amounts to an average of 30 murders, rapes and beatings. The context of the violence was disturbingly similar as well. Most of the depictions CMPA accounted for were glorified and sanitized, with little said or shown about the consequences for victims or perpetrators, which child development experts say is the worst and potentially most harmful signal to send to young viewers.

"The gnawing question we have to ask today is whether the television and movie industry reaction to these findings will also be the same as it has been. If the past few months are any indication, I am not overly optimistic. There has been some progress in the wake of the massacre in Littleton and the public pleas for greater media responsibility, some reflection of heightened sensitivities, a few moves to actually change program content. But sadly these responses amount to little more than window dressing, or in this case screen dressing, especially when compared to the volume of violence we've been swamped with over the last year, as documented in this study. So the challenge now falls to us as consumers, as parents, as grandparents, and as citizens of this democracy. If we want a safer, saner culture, we have to clearly and loudly ask the people who shape it how many more kids must be slaughtered before we wake up to our shared responsibilities to protect them from harmful influences, on screen and off. We have to ask them, particularly the companies making money from the public airwaves, how they are serving the public interest by flooding them with conscienceless killing and demeaning sleaze. We have to ask them how many more sadistic, bloodsoaked video games will be marketed to teenage boys and how many more porn stars will be featured on MTV before someone draws the line. And we have to ask ourselves if we are feeding the degradation of our culture by silently tolerating our children's consumption of this mix of media garbage and poison."

Public Safety

On Regulatory Reform
April 21, 1999

"Let me say at the outset how much I appreciate the efforts you and Senator Levin have made on this proposal over a long period of time. I recognize this measure, S. 746, includes a number of changes made in response to some of the concerns expressed about this bill in the last Congress, and I thank you for that.

"Nevertheless, I remain skeptical about the approach of

this legislation for many of the same reasons I have expressed at earlier hearings. I continue to worry about unintended consequences and unforeseen results. Trying to reform every type of regulation with a single law poses, it seems to me, too high a risk to the public's health and safety.

"As democratically elected representatives, our foremost responsibility to the people we serve is to protect them from harm. This means, among other things, maintaining a strong defense and adequately staffing local police departments. It's our equal responsibility to protect people from breathing polluted air, drinking dirty water, eating contaminated food, working under hazardous conditions and falling prey, in myriad other ways, to consumer fraud.

"There's a very broad consensus in this country, and in this Congress, that transcends party lines for an appropriately active regulatory role for government. I think there is also a consensus on the value of enacting protections in an equitable, efficient and factual way, that's open to as much public understanding and participation as possible. We all support, in a broad sense, regulatory reform. The question is how to achieve it. To me the best way is statute by statute and not across-the-board.

"Allow me to cite a couple of examples of what I believe is the right way to enact regulatory reform. The Safe Drinking Water Act Amendments enacted a few years ago included highly targeted reforms that dealt with features unique to the problem of drinking water quality. Similarly, the Food Quality Protection Act, which focused on reforming the pesticide regulatory program, was narrowly tailored. In both instances, negotiations led to agreements intended to increase future cost-effectiveness while giving EPA the flexibility to address the higher-priority risks to the public. Both bills passed the House and Senate by wide, bipartisan margins.

"Now, by comparison, let me offer an example of how I fear omnibus reform might affect regulation under individual statutes. I'm going to use the program regulating toxic air pollution under the Clean Air Act. In 1990, when we were amending the Act, we recognized that toxic air pollution was not being adequately controlled. Literally thousands of pollution sources were releasing chemicals into the air that were known or suspected causes of cancer, birth defects or other serious health problems. Many of these pollution sources were without controls, partly because it took too long for the agency to research and analyze the risks, as was required by the law. Instead, Congress decided there was already sufficient evidence of risk to justify regulating a list of particularly harmful chemicals, to narrow the field of regulation, and we instructed EPA to set basic standards based on existing technologies, without revisiting the questions of risk that Congress had already settled.

"So, if this bill, S. 746, applied to the air toxics program, I worry that EPA could be required to delay issuing standards for these toxic chemicals until the agency conducted extensive risk assessment for each standard, which was not the intention when we adopted the law.

"Today's witnesses will discuss a number of other examples where S. 746 would affect regulation in ways we may not have intended or anticipated. And as troubled as I am about the examples this Committee will hear today, I am equally concerned about the examples we won't hear about—until it's too late. I think it might be interesting to see a law-by-law survey showing how the law would affect individual programs—whether at EPA, the Nuclear Regulatory Commission, the Food and Drug Administration, the National Highway Traffic Safety Administration, the Federal Aviation Administration, or any other agency.

"We've already enacted a number of across-the-board regulatory reforms in recent years. I'd prefer to give these reforms more time so we can evaluate their effectiveness before we go further.

"Again, I know your intentions are worthy. However, my preference is the step-by-step approach that minimizes risks and unforeseen consequences. I look forward to the testimony today and to working with you, Mr. Chairman and Senator Levin, in pursuing the goal that I know we all share, which is more effective regulation in the public interest."

Religion

Before Congress
At the 48th National Prayer Breakfast
February 8, 2000
as entered into the Congressional Record at the request of
     Hon. Tom Lantos

"Mr. President and Mrs. Clinton, Speaker Hastert, Reverend Clergy, Nuncio Montalvo, Dr. Graham, General and Mrs. Ralston, other head table guests and honored guests in the hall, ladies and gentlemen: To each and every one of you I say, Blessed be they who come in the name of the Lord.

"This morning, in this place, this very temporal city comes together to reach up to touch the timeless. It brings to mind the story of the man who is blessed to be able to speak with G-d, and in awe of the Lord's freedom from human constraints of time and space, he asks: 'Lord, what is a second like to you?'

"And G-d answers, 'A second to me is like a thousand years.'

"The man then asks, 'And Lord, what is a penny like to you?'

"'To me,' the Lord declares, 'a penny is a like a million dollars.'

The man pauses, thinks for a minute, and then asks, 'Lord, would you give me a penny?'

"And G-d answers, 'I will. In a second.'

"I am honored to have been asked to speak to you this morning, but as the story shows, I proceed with a profound sense of my own human limitations."

Social Policy

On the Reintroduction of the Employment Non-Discrimination
     Act
June 24, 1999

"I am proud to join my colleagues Senators Kennedy and Jeffords and Congressmen Shays and Frank in reintroducing the Employment Non-Discrimination Act, and thereby reasserting the American ideals of equal opportunity and fair play.

"The underlying goal of this bill is the same as it has been for the previous incarnations of ENDA that we have introduced in the last several Congresses, which is to protect gay men and lesbians from discrimination in the workplace, and to uphold their right to be judged like any other American on their qualifications for the job.

"What is different today is the climate in which we are operating. The revolting murder of Matthew Shepard in Wyoming, followed by the similarly hateful killing of a gay man in Alabama, has, I believe, heightened the awareness of the American people to the fact that, as tolerant as we have become in so many ways, bigotry remains a real threat to homosexuals in this country, not just to their livelihoods but to their lives.

"These violent acts have dramatized the extreme consequences of the prejudice that motivates discrimination, and remind us of the price we all pay for intolerance, namely the cheapening of our common values and our common belief in the self-evident truth, expressed in the Declaration of Independence, that every American is endowed by our Creator with the right life, liberty, and the pursuit of happiness.

"What is also different today is the recent experience of James Hormel, the business leader whom President Clinton long ago nominated to be his ambassador to Luxembourg, and whose confirmation was blocked for no other reason than he is gay. The Hormel case adds another persuasive argument in support of ENDA, because it underscores the vulnerability of the average worker. Mr. Hormel's opportunity to serve his country was saved by the personal intervention of the President of the United States. But as the victims of discrimination who are here with us can attest, there is no such thing as a recess appointment in the private sector.

"In fact, outside of 11 states, there are no laws to protect gay men and women from being denied a job or a promotion they deserve, or fired from a job they have earned, just because of their sexual orientation. This is unequivocally wrong. It was when we first introduced this legislation, and it remains so today. It runs counter to our constitutional grain. And it offends our most fundamental American values. We are better than that, and it is time to say so in law by finally passing ENDA."

Supporting the Hate Crimes Prevention Act
June 16, 2000

"I support the goals of this law—the federal prosecution of people who inflict serious harm on others because of the color of the victim's face, the sound of the victim's foreign accent, or the name of the victim's religion. In short, these are crimes committed because the victim is different in some way from the perpetrator, and such crimes should be federally prosecuted. But we can and should do more.

"I think we ought to add to the list of motivations gender, sexual orientation, and disability, as provided in the amendment Sen. Kennedy will offer on Monday, and of which I am a co-sponsor. Crimes like that committed against Matthew Shepard, who was killed because he was a gay man, are no less despicable and no less worthy of federal prosecution than are those committed against others currently included in the federal law.

"As the law now stands, it also imposes an unnecessary obstacle to prosecutions relating to race, color, religion, and national origin, in that the law is only triggered if the victim is prevented from exercising a listed federally protected activity. I support the provision of this amendment that would eliminate this obstacle and therefore broaden the ability of federal prosecutors to pursue crimes motivated by racial or religious hatred.

"The Kennedy amendment also includes new language requiring the Justice Department, prior to indicting a defendant in a hate crime, to certify either that the state is not going to prosecute a hate crime, that the state requested or does not object to Justice Department prosecution, or that the state has completed prosecution. This certification provision should satisfy the concerns of any of my colleagues who fear that federal prosecutors will interfere with state efforts to bring perpetrators of hate crimes to justice."

Clinton

On Impeachment Trial of President Clinton
January 15, 1999

"I thought that my colleagues in the Senate were paying close and respectful attention to the House managers as they presented their case yesterday, will do so again today, and will do so next week when the President's counsel begins his arguments.

"I'm taking extensive notes as I think a judge would in listening to a case. I'm writing down questions that I would think of asking if I have the opportunity. We are seeing the adversary process at work. We always believe that truth results from that, and I hope it will here."

Regarding Open Impeachment Deliberations
February 5, 1999

"Only through full and complete access to the deliberations of public officials can citizens make intelligent, informed decisions about the direction of their government and their elected representatives. Nowhere is this principle more important than here and now, when 100 elected Senators are deciding whether to remove a President who has twice won popular election and who still enjoys wide public support. If we close our deliberations at this extraordinary moment in our nation's history, the public will be forever deprived of a full accounting of these proceedings, and some may question our willingness to be held accountable for our actions. For the public to have any faith in the fairness of these impeachment proceedings, it must understand how we conducted our deliberations and what motivated our decisions.

"Senate rules that dictate closed deliberations are outdated and outweighed by a compelling national interest.

"Rather than being shielded from scrutiny, we have an obligation to explain our decisions to the electorate, and our constituents have the right to take those explanations into account when they vote.

"Finally, the public's confidence in government—such as it is—has been further shaken by the events of the past year. We will all have to work hard to regain the public's trust. We can begin now by allowing the American people to see this ugly episode end on a note of rational and thoughtful debate. As a result, the Senate will be able to escape with its dignity intact, and the public will realize that its elected representatives have taken seriously their obligations to render impartial justice."

Gore

Commending Gore's National Retirement Savings Plan
June 20, 2000

"I can't help but admire the details of Al Gore's retirement savings proposal. His clear intention is to provide hard-working, low- and middle-income families an opportunity to boost their savings so they may rest easier in their retirement years, knowing they have worked hard to build real economic security.

"The vice president's idea rightly identifies the potential of the private sector to help us achieve a very public interest. Just as importantly, he makes clear that this is not an empty gesture of a handout today, but an empowerment tool for tomorrow.

"It is a tool that would benefit all of our economy, helping us to restore faith in the longstanding American promise of equal opportunity. That faith lately has been shaken by the disconcerting divisions of income and wealth in our society. The vice president's proposal is an admirable response."

Letter to Janet Reno Urging Internal Investigation of Leaks
*   from the Campaign Finance Investigation involving Vice*
*   President Al Gore*
June 27, 2000

Dear Attorney General Reno,

I am writing to express my very serious concerns about the apparent unauthorized disclosure of information related to the ongoing campaign finance investigation involving Vice President Gore. As I understand this matter, no information related to any Special Counsel recommendation was officially released by the Department. As a former State Attorney General and a Senator involved in past campaign finance investigations, I understand that it is difficult enough to conduct a credible investigation into sensitive political matters of public importance; it is impossible to do so in an atmosphere of leaks of internal investigative documents. I am dismayed that the people responsible for these unauthorized disclosures are willing to threaten the integrity of ongoing investigations in pursuit of their own individual objectives.

Making the decision whether to appoint a Special Counsel is one of the Attorney General's most difficult and important responsibilities. It does a grave disservice to the Attorney General's truth-seeking and law enforcement mission when internal deliberations relating to that mission are leaked. Whether the intention was to bring outside pressure to bear on the decision-making process, or to embarrass one of the possible subjects of the investigation, such unauthorized disclosure is grossly unethical. As you recognize, such disclosures also damage the Department's reputation for objectivity and harm its ability to conduct future high-profile investigations.

I recommend that you consider an internal investigation of this matter and discipline any Department employee you conclude has acted irresponsibly. That is necessary to preserve and protect the independence and integrity of the Department of Justice's investigative work.

Sincerely,
Joseph I. Lieberman

APPENDIX IV

Selections from Senator Lieberman's Voting Record

Senators routinely cast hundreds of votes each year. This annotated version of Senator Lieberman's voting record has been edited to give the reader an overview of his votes. A more inclusive listing may be found at www.vote-smart.org, and complete Congressional Records can be found at www. c-span.org, and www.thomas.loc.gov.

Abortion

September 11, 1991
Bill Number: H.R. 2707, Amendment 1108
Parental Notification
To require entities receiving assistance under title X of the Public Health Service Act to provide for parental notification in the case of minor patients who request an abortion.
Passed; Lieberman voted **YES**

November 7, 1991
Bill Number: H.R. 2707
Departments of Labor, Health and Human Services, and Education, and Related Agencies Appropriations Act, 1992
Prohibits the use of funds to perform abortions except where

the life of the mother would be endangered if the fetus were carried to term. Also prohibits the use of funds to enforce or otherwise implement regulations prohibiting abortion counseling and referral services and limiting program services to family planning.
Passed; Lieberman voted **YES**

March 31, 1992, 6:33 PM
Bill Number: H.R.2507 Amendment Number: S.AMDT.NO. 1749
National Institutes of Health Reauthorization
Bill authorizes appropriations for specified national research institutes and agencies of the National Institutes of Health (NIH); revises certain NIH programs; redesignates specified NIH agencies; modifies NIH administrative requirements; and mandates certain studies and reports. Establishes entities and programs. Establishes a fund for use by the NIH Director to carry out NIH activities. Transfers from the Health Research Extension Act of 1985 to the Public Health Service Act provisions concerning an Alzheimer's disease registry. Amendment provides for the establishment of a physician and hospital registry and a fetal tissue bank, banning tissue gained from induced abortions.
Failed; Lieberman voted **NO**

October 1, 1992
Bill Number: S.323
Family Planning Amendments Act of 1992
Motion to override veto of the bill, which requires federally funded family planning services to provide individuals, on request, information on pregnancy management options, defined as nondirective counseling and referrals regarding prenatal care and delivery; infant care, foster care, and adoption; and termination of pregnancy. Allows a provider who objects, on religious or moral grounds, to providing information on an option to refer the woman to another provider in the

geographic area. Prohibits such assistance unless the provider is in compliance with State law regarding parental notification of or consent for the performance of an abortion on a minor.
Passed; Lieberman voted **YES**

September 28, 1993
Bill Number: H.R. 2518, Amendment 185
Abortion & Family Planning
Departments of Labor, Health and Human Services, and Education, and Related Agencies Appropriations Act, 1994
An amendment to prohibit the use of any funds appropriated in the bill for any abortion except, when it is necessary to save the life of the mother or when the pregnancy is the result of an act of rape or incest.
Rejected; Lieberman voted **YES**

May 12, 1994
Bill Number: S. 636
Abortion Clinic Access Bill
Amends the Federal criminal code to prohibit: (1) intentionally injuring, intimidating, or interfering with, or attempting to injure, intimidate, or interfere with, any person by force, threat of force, or physical obstruction because that person is or has been, or in order to intimidate such person or any other person or any class of persons from, obtaining or providing reproductive health services; (2) intentionally injuring, intimidating, or interfering with, or attempting to injure, intimidate, or interfere with, any person by force, threat of force, or physical obstruction exercising or seeking to exercise the First Amendment right of religious freedom at a place of religious worship; or (3) intentionally damaging or destroying the property of a facility, or attempting to do so, because such facility provides reproductive health services, or intentionally damaging or destroying the property of a place of religious worship.
Passed; Lieberman voted **YES**

August 5, 1995
Bill Number: H.R. 2020
A bill making appropriations for the Treasury Department, the United States Postal Service, the Executive Office of the President, and certain Independent Agencies, for the fiscal year ending September 30, 1996, and for other purposes
Prohibits Act funds being available to pay for an abortion or expenses in connection with any health plan under the Federal employees health benefit program which provides any benefits or coverage for abortions, except where the life of the mother would be endangered if the fetus were carried to term or where the pregnancy is the result of rape or incest.
Passed; Lieberman voted **NO**

December 7, 1995
Bill Number: H.R. 1833
Partial-Birth Abortion Ban Act of 1995
Subjects any physician who knowingly performs a partial-birth abortion in or affecting interstate or foreign commerce to a fine or imprisonment for not more than two years or both, except where such an abortion is necessary to save the life of a mother endangered by a physical disorder, illness, or injury, provided that no other medical procedure would suffice.
Passed; Lieberman voted **NO**

September 26, 1996
Bill Number: H.R. 1833
Override Presidential Veto of Partial Birth Abortion Ban Act of 1997
Failed; Lieberman voted **NO**

May 20, 1997
Bill Number: H.R. 1122
Partial-Birth Abortion Ban Act of 1997
Amends the Federal criminal code to prohibit any physician from knowingly performing a partial-birth abortion in or af-

fecting interstate or foreign commerce, unless it is necessary to save the life of the mother.
Passed; Lieberman voted **NO**

September 11, 1997
Bill Number: S. 1061, Amendment 1077
An original bill making appropriations for the Departments of Labor, Health and Human Services, and Education, and related agencies for the fiscal year ending September 30, 1998, and for other purposes
None of the amounts for the Morris K. Udall Parkinson's Research Act of 1997 may be expended for any research that utilizes human fetal tissue, cells, or organs that are obtained from a living or dead embryo or fetus during or after an induced abortion. This subsection does not apply to human fetal tissue, cells, or organs that are obtained from a spontaneous abortion or an ectopic pregnancy.
Rejected; Lieberman voted **NO**

September 18, 1998
Bill Number: H.R. 1122
Override Presidential Veto of Partial Birth Abortion Ban Act of 1997
Failed; Lieberman voted **NO**

Affirmative Action

July 20, 1995
Bill Number: H.R. 1854, Amendment 1825
A bill making appropriations for the Legislative Branch for the fiscal year ending September 30, 1996, and for other purposes
None of the funds made available by this Act may be used by any unit of the legislative branch of the Federal Government to award any Federal contract, or to require or encourage the award of any subcontract, if such award is based, in whole or

in part, on the race, color, national origin, or gender of the contractor or subcontractor.
Rejected; Lieberman voted **NO**

Agriculture

February 7, 1996
Bill Number: S.1541
Agricultural Market Transition Act of 1996
A Bill to extend, reform, and improve agricultural commodity, trade, conservation, and other programs, and for other purposes. Authorizes the Secretary of Agriculture to enter into production flexibility contracts through crop year 2002 with eligible agricultural operators and owners with respect to conservation, wetlands, and planting flexibility requirements.
Passed; Lieberman voted **YES**

Armed Services

June 25, 1988
Bill Number: S. 2057, Amendment 3011
Strom Thurmond National Defense Authorization Act for Fiscal Year 1999
Amendment to require separate training platoons and separate housing for male and female basic trainees, and to ensure after-hours privacy for basic trainees. Bill includes appropriations for all branches of the armed services.
Passed; Lieberman voted **YES**

July 27, 1989
Bill Number: S.1352, Amendment 500
An original bill to authorize appropriations for fiscal years 1990 and 1991 for military functions of the Department of Defense and to prescribe military personnel levels for such

Department for fiscal years 1990 and 1991, and for other purposes

Motion to table (kill) amendment to reduce funds for the SDI (Strategic Defense Initiative) program and increase funds for certain other programs.

Passed; Lieberman voted **NO**

October 15, 1990
Bill Number: S.3189, Amendment 2992
Department of Defense Appropriations Act, 1991
Amendment to limit the use of funds for the B-2 Advanced Technology Bomber Program. Bill appropriates funds for the Department of Defense.
Failed; Lieberman voted **YES**

July 31, 1991
Bill Number: S.1507, Amendment 957
National Defense Authorization Act for Fiscal Years 1992 and 1993
Amendment revises the strategy for the Strategic Defense Initiative to prevent deployment. Bill authorizes appropriations for military functions of the Department of Defense. Prescribes military personnel levels. Authorizes appropriations for: national security programs of the Department of Energy; civil defense; and the Panama Canal Commission.
Failed; Lieberman voted **YES**

September 18, 1992
Bill Number: S.3114, Amendment 3043
National Defense Authorization Act for Fiscal Year 1993
An Act to authorize appropriations for fiscal year 1993 for military activities of the Department of Defense, for military construction, and for defense activities of the Department of Energy, to prescribe personnel strengths for such fiscal year for the Armed Forces, to provide for defense conversion, and for other purposes. The amendment calls for a 9-month moratorium on nuclear testing.
Passed; Lieberman voted **YES**

September 9, 1993
Bill Number: S.1298, Amendment 785
National Defense Authorization Act for Fiscal Year 1994
Amendment to reduce the amount provided for ballistic missile
defense programs and to allocate the total amount among the
ballistic missile defense programs and program elements.
Passed; Lieberman voted **NO**

September 5, 1995
Bill Number: S.1087
Defense Department FY96 Appropriations Bill
An original Bill making appropriations for the Department of
Defense for the fiscal year ending September 30, 1996, and for
other purposes.
Passed; Lieberman voted **YES**

October 30, 1997
Bill Number: S.1292
Line Item Veto Cancellation bill, also referred to as: *A bill dis-
approving the cancellations transmitted by the President on
October 6, 1997, regarding Public Law 105–45*
Disapproves the President's cancellations (line item veto) of
appropriations for 36 military construction projects in the Mili-
tary Construction Appropriations Act, 1998.
Passed; Lieberman voted **YES**

May 25, 1999
Bill Number: S.1059, Amendment 383
FY2000 Defense Authorization Bill
Motion to table (kill) an amendment to direct the President,
pursuant to the United States Constitution and the War Powers
Resolution, to seek approval from Congress prior to the introduction of ground troops from the United States Armed Forces
in connection with present operations against the Federal Republic of Yugoslavia or funding for that operations will not be
authorized.
Passed; Lieberman voted **YES**

The Arts

September 29, 1989
Bill Number: H.R.3072, Amendment 891
Department of Defense Appropriations Act, 1990
Motion to table (kill) amendment to express the Sense of the
Senate that the conferees on H.R.2788, Department of the Inte-
rior Appropriations, 1990, should insist on amendment number
7, to prohibit the use of appropriated funds for the dissemina-
tion, promotion or production of obscene or indecent materials
denigrating a particular religion.
Passed; Lieberman voted **YES**

September 19, 1991
Bill Number: H.R. 2686
*National Endowment for the Arts (Funding-in Interior Approp-
iations) Bill*, also referred to as: *A bill making appropriations
for the Department of the Interior and related agencies for the
fiscal year ending September 30, 1992, and for other purposes*
To provide that none of the funds made available to the National Endowment for the Arts under this Act may be used to
promote, disseminate, or produce materials that depict or de-
scribe, in a patently offensive way, sexual or excretory activities or organs.
Passed; Lieberman voted **NO**

July 25, 1994
Bill Number: H.R. 4602, re: Amendment 2396
Motion to Table Amendment re: Use of NEA Funds
To table (kill) an amendment brought by Senator Helms which
would prohibit the use of National Endowment for the Arts
funds to provide financial assistance for projects or works involving the mutilation of living or dead human beings, or the
drawing or letting of blood.
Passed; Lieberman voted **YES**

September 15, 1998
Bill Number: S 2237, Amendment 3593
Department of the Interior and Related Agencies Appropriations Act, 1999
To table (kill) an amendment brought by Senator Ashcroft to eliminate funding for the National Endowment for the Arts and to transfer funds for the operation of the National Park System.
Passed; Lieberman voted **YES**

September 17, 1997
Bill Number: H.R. 2107, Amendment 1188
Termination of the National Endowment for the Arts, part of A bill making appropriations for the Department of the Interior and related agencies for the fiscal year ending September 30, 1998, and for other purposes.
To eliminate funding for programs and activities carried out by the National Endowment for the Arts.
Rejected; Lieberman voted **NO**

September 17, 1997
Bill Number: H.R. 2107, Amendment 1187
Hutchinson Amendment
To provide financial assistance to States to support the arts (in place of the NEA).
Rejected; Lieberman voted **NO**

August 5, 1999
Bill Number: H.R. 2466, Amendment 1569
Department of the Interior and Related Agencies Appropriations Act, 2000
To table (kill) an amendment brought by Senator Smith to eliminate funding for the National Endowment for the Arts.
Passed; Lieberman voted **YES**

Budget

June 19, 1991
Bill Number: S.1204, Amendment 358
National Highway Traffic Safety Administration Authorization Act of 1991

Amendment eliminates language which lowers the Federal share payable for certain projects. Act authorizes appropriations from the Highway Trust Fund for surface transportation and other highway programs, the National Traffic and Motor Vehicle Safety Act of 1966, the Motor Vehicle Information and Cost Savings Act, the National Driver Register Act of 1982, and the National Highway Traffic Safety Administration. Establishes a Bureau of Transportation Statistics and the National Recreational Trails Trust Fund. Authorizes grants for commercial motor vehicle safety standards enforcement. Provides for the establishment of drug testing and rehabilitation programs for transportation personnel. Establishes the Rural Tourism Development Foundation.
Passed; Lieberman voted **YES**

July 17, 1991
Bill Number: H.R.2506, Amendment 770
Legislative Branch Appropriations Act, 1992
Amendment provides for an equalization in certain rates of pay, to apply the honoraria ban and the provisions of title V of the Ethics in Government Act of 1978 to Senators and officers and employees of the Senate, and for other purposes. A Bill making appropriations for the Legislative Branch for the fiscal year ending September 30, 1992, and for other purposes.
Passed; Lieberman voted **YES**

September 10, 1991
Bill Number: H.R.2707, Amendment 1083
Departments of Labor, Health and Human Services, and Education, and Related Agencies Appropriations Act, 1992
Amendment increases the amounts made available for disease control, biomedical research, mental health, low-income home energy assistance, legalization assistance grants, Head Start, Chapter I basic grants, and Pell grants, totaling $3.1 billion, offset from defense. Bill making appropriations for the Departments of Labor, Health and Human Services, and Education, and related agencies, for the fiscal year ending September 30, 1992, and for other purposes.
Failed; Lieberman voted **NO**

March 13, 1992
Bill Number: H.R. 4210
Tax Fairness and Economic Growth Act of 1992, also referred
to as: A *bill to amend the Internal Revenue Code of 1986 to
provide incentives for increased economic growth and to provide tax relief for families*
Among the provisions: Amends the Internal Revenue Code to
allow a credit for 20 percent of a taxpayer's social security
taxes, limited to $150 ($300 in the case of a joint return) and
applicable to years beginning after December 31, 1991, and
before January 1, 1994. Increases the earned income tax credit
and repeals its interaction with the medical expense deduction,
the deduction for health insurance costs of the self-employed,
and the supplemental young child credit. Allows a credit for
interest paid or incurred on a qualified education loan for a 48-
month period (whether or not consecutive). Limits such credit
to $400 per individual whose education expenses are being fi-
nanced by such loan. Sets forth limits on the gross income of
taxpayers eligible for such credit.
Passed; Lieberman voted **YES**

March 26, 1992
Bill Number: S.2399
Appropriations Category Reform Act of 1992
States that the Congress declares that it is essential that the
Nation achieve savings in national defense beyond those agreed
to in the budget summit agreement of 1990, reduce the deficit,
and invest in areas of pressing domestic need that have been
neglected since the 1980s. Amends the Congressional Budget
Act of 1974 to revise the discretionary spending limit for FY
1993 by merging the defense and domestic categories into a
national category. Makes conforming changes to the Balanced
Budget and Emergency Deficit Control Act of 1985.
Failed; Lieberman voted **NO**

October 1, 1992
Bill Number: H.R.5368
*Foreign Operations, Export Financing, and Related Programs
Appropriations Act, 1993*

A Bill making appropriations for foreign operations, export financing, and related programs for the fiscal year ending September 30, 1993, and for other purposes.
Passed; Lieberman voted **YES**

April 1, 1993
Bill Number: H.Con.Res. 64
A concurrent resolution setting forth the congressional budget for the United States Government for fiscal years 1994, 1995, 1996, 1997, and 1998
Establishes the budget for FY 1994 and sets forth appropriate budgetary levels for FY 1995 through 1998.
Passed; Lieberman voted **YES**

April 21, 1993
Bill Number: H.R.1335
Emergency Supplemental Appropriations Act of 1993
Motion to limit debate on Emergency Supplemental Appropriations Act of 1993, which makes emergency supplemental appropriations to the Department of Labor for advances to the Unemployment Trust Fund and other funds to remain available until September 30, 1994.
Failed; Lieberman voted **YES**

June 25, 1993
Bill Number: H.R.2264
Omnibus Budget Reconciliation Act of 1993, also referred to as: *Student Loan Reform Act of 1993*
Includes significant money-saving reforms in student loan program rules and establishes group health insurance plan standards; allows a taxpayer other than a corporation to exclude from gross income 50 percent of gain from the sale or exchange of qualified small business stock held for more than five years.
Passed; Lieberman voted **YES**

March 1, 1994
Bill Number: S.J.RES.41
Balanced Budget Amendment to the Constitution
A joint resolution proposing an amendment to the Constitution

of the United States to require a balanced budget. Prohibits in any fiscal year total Federal outlays from exceeding total receipts, unless a three-fifths roll call vote of both Houses of Congress authorizes a specific EXCESS. Prohibits any increases in the public debt unless a three-fifths roll call vote of both Houses enacts legislation permitting otherwise. Directs the President to submit a balanced budget to the Congress. Permits any revenue-increasing bill to become law only if approved by a majority of the whole number of each House by roll call vote. Waives these provisions when a declaration of war is in effect.
Failed; Lieberman voted **NO**

October 27, 1995
Bill Number: H.R.2491
Seven-Year Balanced Budget Reconciliation Act of 1995
A Bill to provide for reconciliation pursuant to section 105 of the concurrent resolution on the budget for fiscal year 1996.
Passed; Lieberman voted **NO**

March 4, 1997
Bill Number: S.J.RES.1
Balanced Budget Amendment to the Constitution
A joint resolution proposing an amendment to the Constitution of the United States to require a balanced budget. Directs the President to submit a balanced budget to the Congress. Authorizes the Congress to waive these provisions when: (1) a declaration of war is in effect; or (2) the United States is engaged in a military conflict which poses a threat to national security as declared by a joint resolution adopted by a majority of each House.
Failed; Lieberman voted **NO**

May 23, 1997
Bill Number: H.CON.RES.84
A concurrent resolution establishing the congressional budget for the United States Government for fiscal year 1998 and

setting forth appropriate budgetary levels for fiscal years 1999, 2000, 2001, and 2002
Budget including Republican-proposed tax cuts and incentives.
Passed; Lieberman voted **YES**

August 3, 1999
Bill Number: S.1233, Amendment 107
Agriculture FY2000 Appropriations Bill
Motion to table (kill) an amendment to provide stability in the United States agriculture sector and to promote adequate availability of food and medicine for humanitarian assistance abroad by requiring congressional approval before the imposition of any unilateral agricultural or medical sanctions against a foreign country or foreign entity.
Failed; Lieberman voted **YES**

Campaign Finance Reform

April 30, 1992
Bill Number: S. 3
Congressional Spending Limit and Election Reform Act of 1993
Amends the Federal Election Campaign Act (FECA) to, among other provisions, treat contributions by a dependent not of voting age as having been made by the individual of whom that person is a dependent. Prohibits a candidate from accepting more than $100 in cash contributions from any one person. Aggregates State and local committee contributions for purposes of political party committee contribution limits. Permits an authorized political committee to contribute up to $10,000 annually to the congressional campaign committees of a political party.
Passed; Lieberman voted **YES**

May 13, 1992
Bill Number: S. 3
Override Presidential Veto of the Above Congressional Spending Limit and Election Reform Act of 1993
Rejected; Lieberman voted **YES**

September 30, 1994
Bill Number: S.3
Congressional Campaign Spending Limit and Election Reform Act of 1993
Motion to limit debate on bill which, among other provisions: Amends Federal Election Campaign Act (FECA) to limit a House of Representatives candidate to accepting in an election cycle not more than $200,000 in aggregate from each of: (1) political parties; and (2) persons other than political parties whose contributions total more than $200.
Failed; Lieberman voted **YES**

October 6, 1994
Bill Number: S.349
Lobbying Disclosure Act of 1993
Motion to limit debate on a bill to provide for the disclosure of lobbying activities to influence the Federal Government, and for other purposes.
Failed; Lieberman voted **YES**

July 25, 1995
Bill Number: S.1060
Lobbying Disclosure Act of 1995
Defines a lobbyist as any individual employed or retained by a client for financial or other compensation for services that include more than one lobbying contact. Requires lobbyists to register with the Secretary of the Senate and the Clerk of the House of Representatives.
Passed; Lieberman voted **YES**

June 25, 1996
Bill Number: S. 1219
Senate Campaign Finance Reform Act of 1995, also referred to as: *A bill to reform the financing of Federal elections, and for other purposes*
Amends Federal Election Campaign Act (FECA) to, among other provisions, prohibit Federal election activities by political

action committees (as defined by this Act). States that if such ban is not in effect: (1) a committee's contributions to a candidate shall not exceed limits applicable to an individual; and (2) a candidate may not accept more than 20 percent of contributions from committee sources. Sets forth reporting requirements for persons other than political parties (with exceptions for candidate's authorized committees or independent expenditures) who disburse more than $2000 for political activities. Requires candidates to raise at least 60 percent of their contributions from in-State individuals in order to be in FECA compliance.
Rejected; Lieberman voted **YES**

March 11, 1997
Bill Number: S.Res. 39
An original resolution authorizing expenditures by the Committee on Governmental Affairs
Amends Senate Resolution 54 (Omnibus Committee Funding Resolution for 1997 and 1998) to authorize supplemental expenditures by the Committee on Governmental Affairs during 1997 for the sole purpose of conducting an investigation of illegal or improper activities in connection with 1996 Federal election campaigns. Directs the Committee to: (1) refer any evidence of such illegal or improper activities involving any Member of the Senate to the Select Committee on Ethics; and (2) submit a final public report of its findings to the Senate by January 31, 1998. Increases the amount authorized for expenditures by the Committee on Rules and Administration for March 1, 1997, through September 30, 1998. Requires such Committee to continue to conduct hearings on campaign reform.
Passed; Lieberman voted **YES**

March 11, 1997
Bill Number: S.Res. 39, Amendment 23
Campaign Finance
Amendment expands above Bill to include "improper" fundraising activities in 1996 federal elections in addition to "illegal" activities.
Passed; Lieberman voted **YES**

March 18, 1997
Bill Number: S. Joint Res. 18
Campaign Finance Reform resolution, also referred to as: *A joint resolution proposing an amendment to the Constitution of the United States relating to contributions and expenditures intended to affect elections*
Constitutional Amendment—Grants authority to: (1) the Congress to set reasonable limits on contributions and expenditures made by, in support of, or in opposition to, a candidate for nomination or election to Federal office; (2) a State to set reasonable limits on contributions and expenditures made by, in support of, or in opposition to, a candidate for nomination or election to State or local office; and (3) the Congress to implement and enforce this amendment by legislation.
Rejected; Lieberman voted **YES**

October 7, 1997
Bill Number: S. 25
Bipartisan Campaign Reform Act of 1997, also referred to as: *A bill to reform the financing of Federal elections*
Vote to end debate on the Bipartisan Campaign Reform Act of 1997, which prohibits Federal election contributions by political action committees (as defined by this Act). States that if such ban is not in effect: (1) a committee's contributions to a candidate shall not exceed limits applicable to an individual; and (2) a candidate may not accept more than 20 percent of contributions from committee sources. Prohibits a national committee of a political party (including specified related entities) from soliciting or receiving soft money contributions.
Rejected; Lieberman voted **NO**

February 25, 1998
Bill Number: S. 1663, Amendment 1646
Paycheck Protection Act, also referred to as: *A bill to protect individuals from having their money involuntarily collected and used for politics by a corporation or labor organization*
Vote to table (kill) McCain Amendment, which included provi-

sion whereby, in the case of an eligible Senate candidate (as defined in section 501 of the Federal Election Campaign Act), the charges for the use of a television broadcasting station during the 30-day period and 60-day period prior to an election shall exceed 50 percent of lowest charge of the station for the same amount of time for the same period on the same date. The bill itself amends the Federal Election Campaign Act to make it unlawful (except with the separate, prior, written, voluntary authorization of a stockholder, employee, member, or non-member) for: (1) national banks or corporations to collect from or assess such stockholder or employee any dues, initiation fee, or other payment as a condition of employment if any part of such dues, fee, or payment will be used for political activities in which the national bank or corporation is engaged; and (2) labor organizations to collect from or assess such member or nonmember any dues, fee, or other payment if any part of such dues, fee, or payment will be used for political activities. States that an authorization shall remain in effect until revoked and may be revoked at any time.
Failed; Lieberman voted **NO**

June 29, 2000
Bill Number: H.R.4762
Political Activities Disclosure
To amend the Internal Revenue Code of 1986 to require 527 organizations to disclose their political activities.
Passed; Lieberman voted **YES**

Chemical Weapons

April 24, 1997
Bill Number: S.Res.75
Chemical Weapons Convention (Ban) Bill, also referred to as: *An executive resolution to advise and consent to the ratification of the Chemical Weapons Convention, subject to certain conditions*

Grants the Senate's advice and consent to the ratification of the Convention on the Prohibition of Development, Production, Stockpiling and Use of Chemical Weapons and on Their Destruction, signed by the United States at Paris on January 13, 1993, including specified protocols and memorandum of understanding (Chemical Weapons Convention), subject to 28 specified conditions, including those summarized below, which shall be binding upon the President.

Passed; Lieberman voted **YES**

Civil Rights

October 24, 1990
Bill Number: S. 2104
Override Presidential Veto of Civil Rights Act of 1990
Amends the Civil Rights Act of 1964 with regard to: (1) disparate impact of employment practices; (2) mixed motive employment discrimination; (3) challenges to practices implementing a judgment or an order; (4) time limits for taking certain actions; (5) seniority systems as a part of collective bargaining agreements; (6) compensatory and punitive damages; (7) declaratory and injunctive relief, and attorney's fees; (8) construction of Federal civil rights laws; and (9) the right to make and enforce contracts.

Provides for the application of specified civil rights Acts to the Congress and certain of its instrumentalities.

Failed; Lieberman voted **YES**

October 30, 1991
Bill Number: S. 1745
Civil Rights Act of 1991
A bill to amend the Civil Rights Act of 1964 to strengthen and improve Federal civil rights laws, to provide for damages in cases of intentional employment discrimination, to clarify provisions regarding disparate impact actions, and for other purposes.

Passed; Lieberman voted **YES**

Crime

June 28, 1991
Bill Number: S.1241, Amendment 503
Violent Crime Control Act of 1991
Amendment proposes compromise language with respect to the purchase of firearms. Bill amends the Omnibus Crime Control and Safe Streets Act of 1968 to authorize appropriations for grants to State and local law enforcement agencies. Amends the Federal criminal code to provide for imposition of the death penalty for specified offenses, to restrict the transfer, importation, receipt, or possession of assault weapons, and to bar application of the exclusionary rule under specified circumstances. Establishes an Office of the Police Corps and Law Enforcement Education within the Department of Justice. Authorizes appropriations for Police Corps and Law Enforcement Scholarship programs. Requires a waiting period and certain documentation prior to the sale, delivery, or transfer of a handgun.
Passed; Lieberman voted **YES**

August 25, 1994
Bill Number: H.R.3355
Violent Crime Control and Law Enforcement Act of 1993
A bill to amend the Omnibus Crime Control and Safe Streets Act of 1968 to allow grants to increase police presence, to expand and improve cooperative efforts between law enforcement agencies and members of the community to address crime and disorder problems, and otherwise to enhance public safety.
Passed; Lieberman voted **YES**

Education

January 23, 1992
Bill Number: S.2, Amendment 1476
Neighborhood Schools Improvement Act
Establishes a National Education Goals Panel and a National

Standards and Assessments Council to support development of
voluntary national education standards and assessment; a
Neighborhood Schools Improvement program of grants for
State and local educational system changes; and a program to
promote flexibility in delivery of education and other services
to disadvantaged children. Amends the General Education Provisions Act to revise provisions for the National Assessment of
Educational Progress. Amends the Carl D. Perkins Vocational
and Applied Technology Education Act to revise provisions for
State use of educational assessment data and for inclusion of
postsecondary education data in occupational information.
Failed; Lieberman voted **YES**

February 8, 1994
Bill Number: H.R.1804
Goals 2000: Educate America Act
A bill to improve learning and teaching by providing a national
framework for education reform; to promote the research, consensus building, and systemic changes needed to ensure equitable educational opportunities and high levels of educational
achievement for all American students; to provide a framework
for reauthorization of all Federal education programs; to promote the development and adoption of a voluntary national system of skill standards and certifications, and for other purposes.
Passed; Lieberman voted **YES**

October 31, 1997
Bill Number: H.R.2646
Parent and Student Savings Account PLUS Act
Motion to limit debate on the bill to amend the Internal Revenue Code of 1986 to allow tax-free expenditures from education individual retirement accounts for elementary and
secondary school expenses, to increase the maximum annual
amount of contributions to such accounts, and for other purposes.
Failed; Lieberman voted **YES**

March 11, 1999
Bill Number: S.280, Amendment 64
Education Flexibility Bill
Motion to table (kill) an amendment to reduce class size, and
for other purposes.
Passed; Lieberman voted **NO**

Employment & the Workplace

October 2, 1991
Bill Number: S.5, Amendment 1245
Family and Medical Leave Act of 1991
Amendment creates the "Family and Medical Leave Act of
1991." Entitles employees to family and temporary medical
leave. Provides for protection of employees' employment and
benefit rights in such cases. Establishes the Commission on
Leave.
Passed; Lieberman voted **YES**

October 1, 1991
Bill Number: S.1722
Emergency Unemployment Compensation Act of 1991
Establishes an emergency unemployment compensation program, and exempts it from orders under the Balanced Budget
and Emergency Deficit Control Act of 1985. Revises provisions for payments of unemployment compensation to former
members of the Armed Forces. Directs the Secretary of Labor
to: establish a demonstration program to provide job search
assistance; establish an Advisory Council on Unemployment
Compensation; report on the method of allocating unemployment compensation program administrative funds among
States; and give special consideration to providing services to
dislocated workers in the States of Washington and Oregon.
Passed; Lieberman voted **YES**

September 24, 1992
Bill Number: S.5
Family and Medical Leave Act of 1991
Override veto of the bill, which entitles employees to 12 work-weeks of leave during any 12-month period because of the birth of their child; the placement of a child for their adoption or foster care; their care of a sick child, spouse, or parent; or their own serious health condition. Provides for protection of employees' employment and benefit rights in such cases. Makes employees eligible for such leave if they have been employed, by the employer from whom leave is sought, for at least a total of 12 months; and 1,250 hours of service during the previous 12-month period. Such coverage is excluded if the employer has less than 50 employees.
Passed; Lieberman voted **YES**

July 2, 1992
Bill Number: H.R.5260
Unemployment Compensation Amendments of 1992
Extends the emergency unemployment compensation (EUC) program. Reduces the maximum number of weeks of EUC benefits for new claimants to 26 (rather than 33) in certain States with high unemployment rates; and 20 (rather than 26) in all other States. Provides for further reduction if the national total unemployment rate falls below certain levels. Modifies EUC eligibility requirements to provide that an individual is not ineligible by reason of subsequent entitlement to regular benefits; and provide certain transition rules, including a waiver of recovery of certain overpayments and an option to defer rights to certain regular benefits.
Passed; Lieberman voted **YES**

February 4, 1993
Bill Number: H.R. 1
Family and Medical Leave Act of 1993
A bill to grant family and temporary medical leave under certain circumstances. Among other provisions, entitles employees to 12 workweeks of leave during any 12-month period

because of: (1) the birth of their child; (2) the placement of a child for their adoption or foster care; (3) their care of a child, spouse, or parent who has a serious health condition; or (4) their own serious health condition which makes them unable to perform the functions of their position.
Passed; Lieberman voted **YES**

September 10, 1996
Bill Number: S.2056
Employment Nondiscrimination Act of 1996
Prohibits employment discrimination on the basis of sexual orientation. Does not apply to the provision of employee benefits for the benefit of an employee's partner. Prohibits quotas and preferential treatment.
Failed; Lieberman voted **YES**

May 15, 1997
Bill Number: S.4
Family Friendly Workplace Act
Motion to limit debate on amendment to the Fair Labor Standards Act of 1938 to provide for, among other provisions: (1) time-and-a-half compensatory time off; (2) biweekly work programs (allowing more than 40 hours of work in one week and correspondingly less in the other); and (3) flexible credit hour programs (thus providing private sector employees opportunities under such programs similar to those enjoyed by Federal employees). Requires, with respect to such compensatory time, biweekly work, and flexible credit hour programs, that employee participation be voluntary, and that collective bargaining agreements be honored.
Failed; Lieberman voted **NO**

Energy

July 10, 1991
Bill Number: H.R.2427, Amendment 686
Energy and Water Appropriations Act, 1992
Amendment prohibits the use of funds for the superconducting super collider. Bill makes appropriations for energy and water

development for the fiscal year ending September 30, 1992, and for other purposes.
Passed; Lieberman voted **YES**

November 1, 1991
Bill Number: S.1220
National Energy Security Act of 1991
Revises national energy security policy with respect to: corporate average fuel economy; fleets and alternative fuels; renewable energy; energy efficiency; oil and gas leasing in the Arctic National Wildlife Refuge; advanced nuclear reactor commercialization; nuclear reactor licensing; uranium; natural gas; the Outer Continental Shelf; research, development, demonstration, and commercialization activities generally; coal, coal technology, and electricity; Public Utility Holding Company Act reform; and the Strategic Petroleum Reserve.
Failed; Lieberman voted **NO**

February 6, 1992
Bill Number: S.2166, Amendment 1576
National Energy Security Act of 1992
Amendment improves the nuclear power plant siting process, and rejects stricter licensing procedures. Bill devises national energy security policy with respect to fleets and alternative fuels; renewable energy; energy efficiency; advanced nuclear reactor commercialization; nuclear reactor licensing; uranium; natural gas; the Outer Continental Shelf; research, development, demonstration, and commercialization activities generally; coal, coal technology, and electricity; Public Utility Holding Company Act reform; the Strategic Petroleum Reserve; stratospheric ozone depletion; and Indian energy resource development.
Passed; Lieberman voted **NO**

August 3, 1994
Bill Number: H.R. 4624, Amendment 2446
Departments of Veterans Affairs and Housing and Urban Development, and Independent Agencies Appropriations Act, 1995

Motion to table (kill) amendment to impose a limitation on the use of funding to promulgate, implement, or enforce an EPA regulation mandating a specified percentage market share for ethanol oxygenates in reformulated gasoline and, in addition, to reduce funding for NASA procurement expenses by $39,300,000.
Passed; Lieberman voted **NO**

Environment

October 21, 1993
Bill Number: H.R.2520
Department of the Interior and Related Agencies Appropriations Act, 1994
Vote to limit debate on the bill, which among other provisions makes appropriations for the Department of Energy for, among other things, fossil energy research and development, the Strategic Petroleum Reserve (SPR), and the SPR Account. Makes appropriations to the Department of Health and Human Services for the Indian Health Service for Indian health services and facilities.
Failed; Lieberman voted **YES**

May 18, 1994
Bill Number: S.2019, Amendment 1720
Safe Drinking Water Act Amendments of 1994
To require risk assessment and cost-benefit analysis regarding major human health or environmental regulations promulgated by the Environmental Protection Agency.
Passed; Lieberman voted **YES**

October 8, 1994
Bill Number: S.21
California Desert Protection Act of 1993
Motion to limit debate on the bill to designate certain lands in the California Desert as wilderness, to establish Death Valley,

Joshua Tree, and Mojave National Parks, and for other purposes.
Passed; Lieberman voted **YES**

July 31, 1996
Bill Number: S.1936
Nuclear Waste Policy Act of 1996
Establishes an integrated management system for spent nuclear fuel and high-level radioactive waste, including its storage, transportation, and disposal. Sets a deadline for development of the capability to commence transfer of waste to the interim storage facility site.
Passed; Lieberman voted **NO**

Federal Assistance Programs

September 19, 1995
Bill Number: H.R.4
Personal Responsibility Act of 1995
Replaces the current Aid to Families with Dependent Children (AFDC) program with a program of block grants to the States for operating statewide temporary assistance (TEA) programs with certain mandatory work, education, and job preparation requirements. Limits such families generally to no more than five years of TEA cash assistance, with certain exceptions. Requires, in addition, certain mandatory adult-supervised living arrangements for unmarried teenage parents. Provides for the exchange of TEA program information with law enforcement agencies under certain conditions.
Passed; Lieberman voted **YES**

August 1, 1996
Bill Number: H.R.3734
Personal Responsibility and Work Opportunity Reconciliation Act of 1996
Replaces the current Aid to Families with Dependent Children

(AFDC) and Job Opportunities and Basic Skills Training (JOBS) programs with a single, combined program of block grants to eligible States with Federal-approved plans for temporary assistance to eligible needy families with a minor child. Eliminates AFDC transitional and at-risk child care programs. Passed; Lieberman voted **YES**

Flag Desecration

June 26, 1990
Bill Number: S.J.RES.332
Flag Desecration Amendment
A joint resolution proposing an amendment to the Constitution of the United States authorizing the Congress and the States to prohibit the physical desecration of the flag of the United States.
Failed; Lieberman voted **NO**

December 12, 1995
Bill Number: S.J.RES.31
Flag Desecration Bill
A joint resolution proposing an amendment to the Constitution of the United States to grant Congress and the States the power to prohibit the physical desecration of the flag of the United States.
Failed; Lieberman voted **NO**

Foreign Policy

January 12, 1991
Bill Number: S.J.RES.2
A joint resolution to authorize the use of United States Armed Forces pursuant to United Nations Security Council Resolution 678
Authorizes the President to use U.S. armed forces to obtain

compliance by Iraq with resolutions adopted by the United Nations Security Council in response to Iraq's aggression against Kuwait.
Passed; Lieberman voted **YES**

July 23, 1991
Bill Number: H.R.2212
United States-China Act of 1991
Sets forth conditions which must be met by China before receiving renewal of nondiscriminatory treatment (most-favored-nation treatment). Terminates most-favored-nation trade status for China if the President determines that it has transferred to Syria or Iran certain ballistic missiles and missile launchers or material and technology which would contribute to the manufacture of a nuclear weapon. Amends the Tariff Act of 1930 to set forth civil penalties for persons who import convict-manufactured goods.
Passed; Lieberman voted **YES**

November 25, 1991
Bill Number: H.R.3807, Amendment 1439
Transfer of Battle Tanks to NATO
Amendment provides for the use of Department of Defense resources for destroying Soviet nuclear and other weapons. Bill amends the Arms Export Control Act to authorize the President to transfer certain defense articles to NATO countries in connection with the Treaty on Conventional Armed Forces in Europe. Provides for the administration and funding of a program to facilitate Soviet weapons destruction. Authorizes emergency airlift of humanitarian assistance, if necessary, to the Soviet Union, its republics, or any successor entities. Authorizes appropriations for the Arms Control and Disarmament Agency and increases the responsibilities of the On-Site Inspection Agency with respect to monitoring nuclear tests.
Passed; Lieberman voted **YES**

July 1, 1992
Bill Number: S.2532, Amendment 2665
Freedom for Russia and Emerging Eurasian Democracies and Open Markets Act
Bill directs the President to designate a coordinator within the Department of State to be responsible for coordinating assistance to the independent states of the former Soviet Union (excluding Estonia, Latvia, and Lithuania). Requires the coordinator to report to the Congress on the overall assistance and economic cooperation strategy for the independent states. Amendment rejects grace period before suspending Russian aid.
Failed; Lieberman voted **YES**

September 23, 1993
Bill Number: H.R.2295
Supplemental Appropriations for the New Independent States of the Former Soviet Union Act, 1993
Provides (1) specified development assistance; (2) international disaster assistance; (3) the Private Sector Revolving Fund; (4) the Foreign Service Retirement and Disability Fund; (5) operating expenses of the Agency for International Development (AID) and the AID Office of Inspector General; (6) worldwide housing guarantees and for administrative expenses of such program; (7) debt restructuring; (8) economic support fund (ESF) assistance; (9) the International Fund for Ireland; (10) economic assistance for Eastern Europe and the Baltic States; (11) assistance for the independent states of the former Soviet Union; (12) the African Development Foundation; (13) the Inter-American Foundation; (14) Overseas Private Investment Corporation direct and guaranteed loans and administrative expenses; (15) the Peace Corps (prohibits the use of such funds for abortions); (16) international narcotics control; (17) migration and refugee assistance; (18) the Emergency Refugee and Migration Assistance Fund; and (19) antiterrorism assistance.
Passed; Lieberman voted **YES**

October 15, 1993
Bill Number: H.R.3116, Amendment 1042
Department of Defense Appropriations Act, 1994
Amendment to provide funding for the involvement of the United States Armed Forces in Somalia through March 31, 1994, unless the President requests and the Congress authorizes an extension of that date, and providing that the United States Armed Forces should remain deployed in or around Somalia until such time as all American service personnel missing in action in Somalia are accounted for, and all American service personnel held prisoner in Somalia are released.
Passed; Lieberman voted **YES**

January 27, 1994
Bill Number: S.1281, Amendment 1263
Foreign Relations Authorization Act, Fiscal Years 1994 and 1995
Amendment to more precisely word the amendment stating the sense of the Senate that in order to maintain and expand further U.S. and Vietnamese efforts to obtain the fullest possible accounting of American servicemen unaccounted for during the war in Vietnam, the President should lift the U.S. trade embargo against Vietnam immediately.
Passed; Lieberman voted **YES**

June 29, 1994
Bill Number: H.R.4426, Amendment 2117
Foreign Operations, Export Financing, and Related Programs Appropriations Act, 1995
Amendment to bill stating that none of the funds appropriated or otherwise made available to the Department of Defense for fiscal year 1995 under this or any other Act may be obligated or expended for any United States military operations in Haiti unless, among other requirements, such operations are authorized in advance by the Congress.
Failed; Lieberman voted **NO**

July 1, 1994
Bill Number: S.2182, Amendment 1851
National Defense Authorization Act for Fiscal Year 1995
To terminate the United States arms embargo applicable to the Government of Bosnia and Herzegovina.
Failed; Lieberman voted **YES**

July 26, 1995
Bill Number: S.21
Bosnia and Herzegovina Self-Defense Act of 1995
Directs the President to terminate the U.S. arms embargo of the Government of Bosnia and Herzegovina following either a request from the Government of Bosnia and Herzegovina for termination of such embargo and the departure of UNPROFOR, or a decision to withdraw UNPROFOR from Bosnia and Herzegovina.
Passed; Lieberman voted **YES**

March 5, 1996
Bill Number: H.R.927
Cuba Sanctions bill
A Bill to seek international sanctions against the Castro government in Cuba, to plan for support of a transition government leading to a democratically elected government in Cuba, and for other purposes.
Passed; Lieberman voted **YES**

March 26, 1998
Bill Number: S.1768, Amendment 2100
An original bill making emergency supplemental appropriations for recovery from natural disasters, and for overseas peacekeeping efforts, for the fiscal year ending September 30, 1998, and for other purposes
Amendment to provide supplemental appropriations of more than $17.3 billion for loans to the International Monetary Fund for the fiscal year ending September 30, 1998, and for other purposes.
Passed; Lieberman voted **YES**

July 15, 1998
Bill Number: X.2159, Amendment 3156
To provide a framework for consideration by the legislative and executive branches of unilateral economic sanctions in order to ensure coordination of United States policy with respect to trade, security, and human rights
Motion to table (kill) above amendment, which would limit the ability of the President to impose sanctions without coordinating policy with Congress.
Passed; Lieberman voted **YES**

Gays in the Military

February 4, 1993
Bill Number: S.5, Amendment 19
Family and Medical Leave Act of 1993
Motion to table (kill) amendment providing that, among other provisions, a thorough review of all Executive orders, Department of Defense directives, and regulations of the military departments concerning the appointment, enlistment, and induction, and the retention, of homosexuals in the Armed Forces of the United States, shall be conducted by the Congress before July 15, 1993. All Executive orders, Department of Defense directives, and regulations of the military departments concerning the appointment, enlistment, and induction, and the retention, of homosexuals in the Armed Forces of the United States, as in effect on January 1, 1993, shall remain in effect until the completion of this review with respect to the Army, Navy, Air Force, and Marine Corps and unless changed by law.
Passed; Lieberman voted **YES**

September 9, 1993
Bill Number: S.1298, Amendment 783
National Defense Authorization Act for Fiscal Year 1994
It is the sense of Congress that the policy of the Government concerning the service of homosexuals in the Armed Forces is

a matter that should be determined by the President, as chief executive officer of the Government and commander-in-chief of the Armed Forces, based upon advice provided to the President by the Secretary of Defense and the military advisors to the President and Secretary.

Failed; Lieberman voted **YES**

Gun Control

May 23, 1990
Bill Number: S.1970, Amendment 1681
Federal Death Penalty Act of 1989
Amendment to strike the gun provisions from the bill. These provisions included prohibition on the sale, shipment, or delivery (or purchase, possession, or acceptance of delivery) of an assault weapon to (or by) any person who does not fill out a specified form.

Failed; Lieberman voted **NO**

November 17, 1993
Bill Number: S.1607, Amendment 1152
Violent Crime Control and Law Enforcement Act of 1993
Amendment to restrict the manufacture, transfer, and possession of certain semiautomatic assault weapons and large capacity ammunition feeding devices.

Passed; Lieberman voted **YES**

November 20, 1993
Bill Number: H.R.1025
The Brady Bill
Amends the Federal criminal code to: (1) require the Attorney General, within five years, to establish a national instant criminal background check system for firearm licensees to contact for information on whether receipt of a firearm by a prospective transferee would violate Federal or State law; and (2) establish an interim five-day waiting period for handgun purchases and

procedures for checking with the chief law enforcement officer of the place of residence of the purchaser (police official) for such information.
Passed; Lieberman voted **YES**

May 20, 1999
Bill Number: S.254, Amendment 362
Juvenile Justice bill
Motion to adopt an amendment to regulate the sale of firearms at gun shows.
Passed; Lieberman voted **YES**

Immigration

May 18, 1998
Bill Number: S.1723
American Competitiveness Act
A bill to amend the Immigration and Nationality Act to assist the United States to remain competitive by increasing the access of the United States firms and institutions of higher education to skilled personnel and by expanding educational and training opportunities for American students and workers.
Passed; Lieberman voted **YES**

Impeachment

February 12, 1999
Motion to remove President Clinton from office under Article I of impeachment, grand jury perjury
Failed; Lieberman voted **NO**

Line Item Veto

March 23, 1995
Bill Number: S.4
Line-Item Veto Bill
An act to give the President line item veto authority with respect to appropriations, new direct spending, and limited tax benefits.
Passed; Lieberman voted **YES**

March 28, 1996
Bill Number: S.4
Line-Item Veto Bill
See above.
Passed; Lieberman voted **YES**

Medicare

June 24, 1997
Bill Number: S.947, Amendment 440
An original bill to provide for reconciliation pursuant to section 104(a) of the concurrent resolution on the budget for fiscal year 1998
Motion to table (kill) amendment to apply the Medicare means testing requirements for part B premiums to individuals with adjusted gross incomes in excess of $100,000 as enacted under section 5542 of this Act, to United States Senators with respect to their employee contributions under the Federal Employees Health Benefits Program.
Passed; Lieberman voted **YES**

National Service

August 3, 1993
Bill Number: H.R.2010
National and Community Service Act of 1993
A bill to amend the National and Community Service Act of 1990 to establish a Corporation for National Service, enhance opportunities for national service, and provide national service educational awards to persons participating in such service, and for other purposes.
Passed; Lieberman voted **YES**

Public Land Use

October 8, 1992
Bill Number: H.R.429
Reclamation Projects Authorization and Adjustment Act of 1992
Revises existing law to allow construction of power generating facilities at Buffalo Bill Dam and Reservoir, Wyoming. Authorizes the construction of recreational facilities in excess of the amount required to replace or relocate existing facilities. Provides that the costs of such construction shall be borne equally by the United States and Wyoming. Authorizes additional appropriations for the Colorado River water storage project (CRSP), to be available solely for design, engineering, and construction of the facilities identified in this title, the planning and implementation of certain fish and wildlife and recreation mitigation and conservation projects and studies, and the Ute Indian Rights Settlement authorized under this Act. Earmarks specified amounts of such additional funds for various reclamation projects and features within Utah. Permits counties in which such projects and features were proposed to be located to participate in certain local development projects.
Passed; Lieberman voted **YES**

September 14, 1993
Bill Number: H.R.2520, Amendment 891
Department of the Interior and Related Agencies Appropriations Act, 1994
Amendment to prohibit the use of funds to implement the Rangeland Reform '94 program.
Passed; Lieberman voted **NO**

Public Safety

June 29, 1994
Bill Number: S.687
Product Liability Fairness Act
Motion to limit debate on a bill to regulate interstate commerce

by providing for a uniform product liability law, and for other purposes. Includes provisions for expedited settlement procedures and civil actions against manufacturers or product sellers.
Failed; Lieberman voted **YES**

March 21, 1996
Bill Number: H.R.956
Product Liability Bill
A Bill to establish legal standards and procedures for product liability litigation, and for other purposes. Allows punitive damages, as permitted by State law. Limits the punitive damage amounts that may be awarded to a claimant, allowing a court to override the limits in certain circumstances. Sets a special lower limit for individuals with a net worth under a specified amount or businesses with fewer than a specified number of employees.
Passed; Lieberman voted **YES**

Nominations

October 2, 1990
Nomination of David H. Souter to be Associate Justice of the U.S. Supreme Court
Confirmed; Lieberman voted **YES**

October 15, 1991
Nomination of Clarence Thomas to be Associate Justice of the U.S. Supreme Court
Confirmed; Lieberman voted **NO**

November 5, 1991
Nomination of Robert M. Gates to be Director of Central Intelligence Agency
Confirmed; Lieberman voted **YES**

August 3, 1993
Nomination of Ruth Bader Ginsberg to be Associate Justice of the U.S. Supreme Court
Confirmed; Lieberman voted **YES**

Taxes

September 25, 1992
Bill Number: H.R.11, Amendment 3181
Revenue Act of 1992
Amendment reduces enterprise zones and IRA deductions in the act, which establishes a demonstration program of providing incentives for the creation of tax enterprise zones in order to revitalize economically and physically distressed areas; promote meaningful employment for zone residents; and encourage individuals to reside in the zones in which they are employed.
Failed; Lieberman voted **NO**

Telecommunications

October 5, 1992
Bill Number: S.12
Cable Television Consumer Protection Act of 1991
Requires each cable operator to offer its subscribers a separately available basic service tier to which the minimum rates shall apply and to which subscription is required for access to all other tiers of service. Prohibits (with exceptions) a cable operator from requiring subscription to any tier other than the basic service tier as a condition of access to cable programming offered on a per channel or per program basis; or discriminating between subscribers to the basic service tier and other subscribers with respect to rates charged for video programming offered on a per channel or per program basis.
Passed; Lieberman voted **YES**

February 1, 1996
Bill Number: S.652
Telecommunications Competition and Deregulation Act of 1995
An original Bill to provide for a pro-competitive, de-regulatory national policy framework designed to accelerate rapidly private sector deployment of advanced telecommunications and information technologies and services to all Americans by opening all telecommunications markets to competition, and for other purposes.
Passed; Lieberman voted **YES**

Tobacco

June 17, 1998
Bill Number: S.1415
A bill to reform and restructure the processes by which tobacco products are manufactured, marketed, and distributed, to prevent the use of tobacco products by minors, to redress the adverse health effects of tobacco use, and for other purposes
Cloture motion: to limit debate on the above, which would place restrictions on the manufacture, advertisement, and distribution of tobacco products.
Cloture motion failed; Lieberman voted **YES**

Trade

November 20, 1993
Bill Number: H.R.3450
North American Free Trade Agreement (NAFTA)
Lowers trade barriers among the United States, Canada and Mexico.
Passed; Lieberman voted **YES**

November 4, 1997
Bill Number: S. 1269
Reciprocal Trade Agreements Act of 1997, also referred to as:
An original bill to establish objectives for negotiating and procedures for implementing certain trade agreements
Motion to proceed with bill that, among other provisions, sets forth the authority of the President to enter trade agreements with foreign countries regarding tariff and non-tariff barriers. States that a trade agreement may be entered only if it makes progress in meeting the applicable objectives, and the President satisfies certain congressional consultation requirements. Authorizes both Houses of Congress to adopt, within 60 days of each other, a procedural disapproval resolution denying fast-track to any trade agreement if the President has failed or refused to notify or consult with the Congress.
Passed; Lieberman voted **YES**

May 11, 2000
Bill Number: H.R.434
Africa Free Trade Bill
An act to authorize a new trade and investment policy for sub-Sahara Africa, expand trade benefits to the countries in the Caribbean Basin, renew the generalized system of preferences, and reauthorize the trade adjustment assistance programs.
Passed; Lieberman voted **YES**

Voter Registration

March 17, 1993
Bill Number: H.R.2
National Voter Registration Act of 1993, also referred to as:
Motor Voter Registration Bill
Requires each State to establish Federal election voter registration procedures by: (1) application made simultaneously with

a driver's license application; (2) mail; and (3) application in person at a designated Federal, State, or nongovernmental office, or at the applicant's residential registration site in accordance with State law.

Passed; Lieberman voted **YES**

Bibliography

Barone, Michael & Ujifusa, Grant, *The Almanac of American Politics 2000*, Times Books, 2000.

Bowles, Chester, *Promises to Keep*, Harper & Row, 1971.

Connecticut Humanities Council, *An Orderly and Decent Government*.

Faude, Wilson H., *Hartford*, Arcadia, 1994.

Grant, Marion Hepburn, *In and about Hartford*, The Connecticut Historical Society,1989.

Halberstam, David, *The Fifties*, Villard Books, 1993.

Jacobs, Jane, *The Death and Life of Great American Cities*, Vintage Books, 1992.

Lieberman, Joseph, *In Praise of Public Life*, Simon & Schuster, 2000.

Michelin, *The Green Guide: Yale University and New Haven*, Michelin Travel Publications, 2000.

Muller, Herbert J., *The Uses of the Past: Profiles of Former Societies*, A Mentor Book, 1952.

Robinson, George, *Essential Judaism: A Complete Guide to Beliefs, Customs, and Rituals*, Pocket Books, 2000.

Schlesinger, Arthur M., Jr., *Robert Kennedy and His Times*, Houghton Mifflin, 1978.

Turque, Bill, *Inventing Al Gore*, Houghton Mifflin, 2000.

Weicker, Lowell P., *Maverick: A Life in Politics*, Little, Brown & Co., 1995.

White, Theodore H., *The Making of the President 1960*, Buccaneer Books, 1961.

Woodward, Bob, *The Choice*, Simon & Schuster, 1996.

Zelnick, Bob, *Gore: A Political Life*, Regenery, 1999.

Ziffer, Amy, *The Connecticut Guide*, Fulcrum Publishing, 1998.

Bibliography of Periodicals

Associated Press, "A Hate Speech Vigil Online," August 10, 2000.

Associated Press, "Lieberman's Neighbors See No Big Election Problem with Religion," Adam Gorlick, August 7, 2000.

Associated Press, "Lieberman's Wife Keeps him a 'Regular Joe,'" August 9, 2000.

Bloomberg News, "Gore's Lieberman Choice Has Its Risks," Paul Alexander, August 10, 2000.

Broadcasting & Cable, " 'It's Unacceptable,' " Sen. Joseph Lieberman [interview], May 17, 1999.

Broadcasting & Cable, "Critics See NBC Behaving Badly," Heather Fleming, May 19, 1997.

Broadcasting & Cable, "Talk Targeters Name Names," Christopher Stern, December 11, 1995.

Bucks County Courier-Times, "Focus on Religious Background Frivolous," David Broder, August 10, 2000.

Buffalo News, Buffalo, N.Y., "The Lieberman Factor," August 9, 2000.

CFO, "Regulating the Regulators," Lauren John, December 1994.

Chicago Sun-Times, "Meet the Liberal Centrist," Dennis Byrne, August 9, 2000.

Chicago Sun-Times, "Moderate Talk, but a Distinctly Liberal Walk," Robert Novak, August 10, 2000.

Chicago Tribune, "Lieberman's Politics, Not His Faith, Should Matter More to U.S." John Kass, August 9, 2000.

Chicago Tribune, "Will Lieberman Hang in There?" Daniel T. Zanoza, August 11, 2000.

Christian Science Monitor, "How to Mend America's Broken Urban Areas: A bipartisan plan would replace bureaucracy with incentives to families, business, and faith-based groups," Joseph Lieberman, May 20, 1997.

Christian Science Monitor, "Meeting the Most Serious Environmental Issue Solutions Could Include Energy Efficient Technologies, Incentives for Conservation, and Reduced Energy Subsidies," Joseph Lieberman, April 24, 1997.

Connecticut Post, "Devoted Followers Brave Heat, Throng to See Native Son," Marian Gail Brown, August 10, 2000.

Connecticut Post, "Gore Joins Lieberman in Stamford Spotlight," Ken Dixon, August 10, 2000.

Connecticut Post, "Hour of Power," Ken Dixon, August 9, 2000.

ctnow.com, "During Private Law Career, Lieberman Courted Politics," Adam Gorlick, August 8, 2000.

ctnow.com., "Lieberman in Connecticut: A Chronology," John Springer, August 8, 2000.

Dallas Morning News, "Gore Picks Lieberman as Running Mate," G. Robert Hillerman, August 7, 2000.

Economist, "Fear in Connecticut," anonymous, October 29, 1988.

Economist, ". . . Fear in Connecticut," October 29, 1988.

Electronic News, "Senator Picks Semiconductors to Prove a Point," Joseph I. Lieberman [interview], May 12, 1997.

Hartford Courant, "America Meets Joe," David Lightman, August 9, 2000.

Hartford Courant, "Candidates Histories Converge in Visits," Lisa Chedekel et al., August 10, 2000.

Hartford Courant, "Media Focus on Faith May Fade," Tara Weiss and David Daley, August 9, 2000.

Hartford Courant, "New Guys on Lieberman's Block," William Weir, August 9, 2000.

Hartford Courant, "Religion: A Barrier Is Broken, and Community's Joy Merges with Fear," Janice D'Arcy, August 8, 2000.

Hartford Courant, "The Team Player," David Lightman and Lisa Chedeckel, August 10, 2000.

Hartford Courant, "Thanking Her Town," Lynne Tuohy and Jane Dee, August 11, 2000.

Hartford Courant, "The South: Speech in Nashville Highlights the Issue of Religion," Lisa Chedekel, August 9, 2000.

Hartford Courant, "With Lieberman's Rise, the Scrutiny Begins," David Lightman, August 9, 2000.

Houston Chronicle, "Lieberman Moderate? Not the Real Joe," Robert D. Novak, August 10, 2000.

Houston Chronicle, "Lieberman Part of a New Alliance across the Lines," Senator Sam Brownback, August 10, 2000.

Houston Chronicle, "Lieberman's Faith Shouldn't Be an Issue of Concern . . . But His Scattered Political Philosophy May Be," Michele Jacklin, August 9, 2000.

Houston Chronicle, "No Doubt Where Lieberman Calls Home," William F. Buckley, Jr., August 12, 2000.

HR Focus, "Pressure Mounts against New Reporting Rules," Larry Reynolds, March 1994.

Insight on the News, "Hollywood Envelope Pushers Got Their Just Deserts in 1996," L. Brent Bozell III, February 3, 1997.

Jewish World Review, "Religion in Politics, Jewish-Style," Jonathan Tobin, August 11, 2000.

Litchfield County Times, "Gore's Choice of 'a Regular Guy' Applauded Throughout County," Jennifer A. Payton, August 10, 2000.

Los Angeles Times, "A New Era for Social Advocacy?" Brian Lowry, December 15, 1998.

Los Angeles Times, "Gore's Counterweight," August 8, 2000.

Los Angeles Times, "Jewish Leaders Quibble about Epochal Movement," Lynn Smith and Mary Rourke, August 11, 2000.

Los Angeles Times, "Senator's Life Took Same Path as His Faith," Geraldine Baum with Mark Z. Barabak, August 9, 2000.

Los Angeles Times, "Religion Is Not an Issue in Politics," Reverend Edward C. Martin, August 12, 2000.

Management Accounting, "New Bill on Stock Option Accounting," Stephen Barian, September 1993.

National Journal, "Sen. Joseph I. Lieberman, D-Conn.," anonymous, June 14, 1997.

National Review, "Politics: The Challenger's Plight," William F. Buckley, Jr., October 14, 1988.

National Review, "Weicker Watch," anonymous, November 7, 1988.

New Haven Register, "A Life-Changing Moment in Time," Mark Zaretsky, August 8, 2000.

New Haven Register, "Candidate's Wife Values Family, Faith," Carrie Melago, August 9, 2000.

New Haven Register, "Law Partner Recalls Political Dreams," Natalie Missakian, August 9, 2000.

New Haven Register, "Lieberman, First Wife Split Amicably," Susan A. Zavadsky, August 9, 2000.

New Haven Register, "Protest, 'Zanies' Part of the Yale Years," Walter Kita, August 8, 2000.

New Haven Register, "Rebuke Put Clinton Pal in Spotlight," Lolita C. Baldor, August 8, 2000.

New Haven Register, "Running Fiercely from the Start," Gregory B. Hladky, August 8, 2000.

New Haven Register, "VP Choice Source of Pride for Area Jews," Natalie Missakian, August 8, 2000.

New London Day, "Lieberman Hailed in Hometown," Susan Haigh, August 10, 2000.

New London Day, "Lieberman's Orthodoxy and the Role of Women," Steven Slosberg, August 8, 2000.

New London Day, "Non-issues Cloud Gore, Lieberman," Charles E. Potter, Jr., August 12, 2000.

New London Day, "Why Gore Needs Lieberman," Editorial, August 7, 2000.

New Yorker, "The Critic's Chronicles, Part One," Kenneth Tynan Diaries, August 7, 2000.

New York Daily News, "Guided by His Conscience," Richard Cohen, August 9, 2000.

New York Post, "Can Lieberman's Morals Boost Gore?" William F. Buckley, Jr., August 9, 2000.

New York Post, "Cracking the Stereotype," Eric Fetterman, August 9, 2000.

New York Post, "Gore 2000 Looks Like Bush 1988," E. J. Dionne, August 12, 2000.

New York Post, "The Hero Comes Home," William F. Buckley, Jr., August 12, 2000.

New York Post, "Holocaust Horror Inspires Hadassah," Marilyn Rauber, August 9, 2000.

New York Post, "Lieberman Takes a Day of Rest," Vincent Morris, August 12, 2000.

New York Post, "Lieberman's Flip-Flops Leave Blacks Behind," J. Kenneth Blackwell, August 13, 2000.

New York Post, "Religiousness and the Masses," Garry Wills, August 12, 2000.

New York Post, "White House Nervous as Lieberman Eyes 'Lies,' " Deborah Orin, March 19, 1999.

New York Times, "A Bold Move for Identity," Richard L. Berke, August 8, 2000.

New York Times, "A Charmer Who Became a Senator," Paul Zielbauer, August 9, 2000.

New York Times, "Companies Join Big-Donor List for Democrats," John M. Broder and Richard A. Oppel, Jr., August 13, 2000.

New York Times, "Connecticut Q&A: Senator Joseph I. Lieberman; What, He Asks, Are the Children Viewing?" Robert A. Hamilton, January 28, 1996.

New York Times, "Democratic Senator in Finance Hearings Stays above the Fray," Melinda Henneberger, July 29, 1997.

New York Times, "Essay: Two Kangaroo Tickets," William Safire, August 10, 2000.

New York Times, "Hometown Gets a Day to Cheer," David M. Herszenhorn, August 10, 2000.

New York Times, "In Selecting a No.2, No Detail Too Small," David Barstow, August 9, 2000.

New York Times, "Just Red, White and Blue," Laurie Goodstein, August 13, 2000.

New York Times, "Lieberman Is Recalled as a Charmer," Paul Zielbauer, August 9, 2000.

New York Times, "Lieberman's Political Life an Open Book," Alison Mitchell, August 9, 2000.

New York Times, "Moguls Rattled by Gore's Choice of Critic of Entertainment Industry," Bernard Weinraub, August 11, 2000.

New York Times, "Mrs. Lieberman's Story and Others,'" Joseph Berger, August 12, 2000.

New York Times, "The Lieberman Candidacy," Editorial, August 8, 2000.

New York Times, "The 2000 Campaign: The Vice President; Gore and Advisers Gather to Select a Running Mate," Katharine Q. Seelye, August 7, 2000.

New York Times, "Thunder in the Senate," October 8, 1997.

New York Times, "Two Kangaroo Tickets," William Safire, August 10, 2000.

Newsday, "Gore Gets His Man," William Douglas, August 8, 2000.

Newsday, "Lieberman Helps Shift Democrats toward the Center," Editorial, August 10, 2000.

Newsday, "Lieberman's Path Blazed by Ribicoff," Dennis Duggan, August 12, 2000.

Post—Standard, Syracuse, N.Y., "Clear-Cut Choices: National Tickets May Look Alike, but Offer Voters Sharp Contrasts in Substance," August 9, 2000.

Salon, "The Two Faces of Joseph Lieberman," Bruce Shapiro, August 8, 2000.

San Francisco Examiner, "Great Ticket, Bad Button," Rob Morse, August 8, 2000.

Slate, "I Want to Believe," Dahlia Lithwick, August 4, 2000.

Stamford Advocate, "40 Years Ago, a Graduate's Call to Battle Bigotry," August 10, 2000.

Stamford Advocate, "He's Coming Home," Michael Howerton, August 9, 2000.

Stamford Advocate, "Lieberman Holds Court in Stamford," Thomas McFeeley, August 10, 2000.

Stamford Advocate, "LIEBERMANIA! Stamford Welcomes Home a Favorite Son," Gregory B. Hladky, August 10, 2000.

Stamford Advocate, "Local Reactions: Lieberman had Makings of Leader Since High School, Jonathan Lucas and Michael Howerton, August 8, 2000.

Stamford Advocate, "Marcia Lieberman, A Natural in the Limelight," Jonathan Lucas, August 11, 2000.

Stamford Advocate, "A Mother Welcomes Her Son Home," Jonathan Lucas, August 10, 2000.

USA Today, "Label Games—or Else," Joseph Lieberman, December 6, 1993.

USA Today, "Once Again, It's the Economy," Richard Benedetto, August 12, 2000.

USA Today, "Senate Flexes for '88: Several Republicans Face Uphill Battles for Re-election," Bob Minzeseimer, May 4, 1988.

USA Today, "Senator Keeps His Faith at Center of Life in Politics," Andrea Stone, August 8, 2000.

USA Today, "Senators Seek Ratings for Video Games," Mike Snider, December 10, 1993.

Variety, "Orthodox Solution to TV Content," Christopher Stern, May 12, 1997.

Village Voice, "Mondo Washington: Gore's Rabbi," James Ridgeway, August 9–15, 2000.

Wall Street Journal, "Close Senate Race in Connecticut Has a Bear Growling—but Is It Really Sen. Weicker? And Aren't He and Rival in the Wrong Parties?" James M. Perry, November 3, 1988.

Wall Street Journal, "Democrats Deal to Gain Votes for Deficit Bill—Small-Business Tax Break Grows, Medicare Cuts Shrink to Win Backing," Jackie Calmes, June 25, 1993.

Wall Street Journal, "Democrats Hold On to Decisive Control of Congress and Add to Their Strength in Nation's State-houses," David Rogers and David Shribman, November 9, 1988.

Wall Street Journal, "Lieberman: What's Not to Like? Al Gore's running mate has set himself apart from his party. If only he were more of a fighter," by Seth Lipsky, August 9, 2000.

Wall Street Journal, "Way Ahead in Connecticut, Sen. Lieber-man Preaches the Virtues of Moderation to Democrats," Dennis Farney, October 28, 1994.

Washington Post, "Abraham Ribicoff, 87, Dies," Martin Weil, February 23, 1998.

Washington Post, "Buckley's for Lieberman, Believe it or Not," Maralee Schwartz, August 16, 1988.

Washington Post, "The Bureaucrat vs. the Risk-Taker," David Maraniss and Ellen Nakashima, August 12, 2000.

Washington Post, "Dirty Air Isn't Free, Either," Joseph Lieber-man [letter], June 18, 1989.

Washington Post; "Faith-Based Campaigning," August 10, 2000.

Washington Post, "Gore Trims His Running Mate List; Attention Focuses on Several Baby Boomer Senators, 'Wild Card' Candidate," Ceci Connolly, August 3, 2000.

Washington Post, "Hadassah Lieberman Exhibits Political Caution, Commitment," Susan Schmidt, August 9, 2000.

Washington Post, "Humbling Dilemma for an Undecided Senator," Guy Gugliotta, October 16, 1991.

Washington Post, "In Completing Ticket, Gore Showed Will—And Willingness to Take Risk," Mark Allen and Dan Balz, August 10, 2000.

Washington Post, "In Connecticut, Rebellious Republicans," George F. Will, October 27, 1988.

Washington Post, "In Lieberman's Orthodoxy, a Special Significance for Jews," Hanna Rosin, August 9, 2000.

Washington Post, "Integrity on the Ticket," August 8, 2000.

Washington Post, "The Reality behind Clinton's Rosy View," Hobart Rowen, July 10, 1994.

Washington Post, "Reverse Gridlock?" Hobart Rowen, November 10, 1994.

Washington Post, "Same Data, Different Conclusions: The Elusive Energy Consensus," Thomas W. Lippman, November 4, 1991.

Washington Post, "The Thinking Person's Choice," George F. Will, August 8, 2000.

World Wastes, "Bill to Promote Environmental Technologies," Cathy Dombowski, August 1993.

Bibliography of Transcripts

Burden of Proof, CNN, "Will Gore-Lieberman Ticket Impact the Law?" Prof. Akil Amar, Daniel Marley, Richard Blumenthal, Clarine Nardi Riddle.

Crossfire, CNN, "What does Joe Lieberman Bring to the Democratic Ticket?"

Larry King Live, CNN, "What Does Joseph Lieberman Bring to the Democratic Ticket? Sen. Barbara Boxer, George McGovern, Michael Dukakis, Senator Charles Schumer, Bob Woodward, August 7, 2000.

Meet the Press, debate between Sen. Joseph Lieberman and Pat Buchanan, April 25, 1999.

Newshour with Jim Lehrer, PBS, interview with Sen. Lugar, Sen. Brownback, Congresswoman Cynthia McKinney, and Senator Joseph Lieberman, February 10, 1998.

Newshour with Jim Lehrer, PBS, "Newsmaker" interview with Sen. Bob Dole, April 17, 1996.

TalkBack Live, CNN, "Will Joe Lieberman Make the Democrats the Ticket to Ride?" August 7, 2000.

Useful Websites

www.ABCNews.com

www.about.com

www.adl.org (The Anti-Defamation League)

www.AlGore2000.com

www.AOL.com

www.cnn.com

www.encyclopedia.com

www.everythingjewish.com

www.jewish.com

www.msn.com

www.policy.com

www.polyconomics.com

www.religioustolerance.com

www.rollcall.com

www.salon.com

www.wiesenthal.com (The Simon Wiesenthal Center)